Empowerment Program

JENNY KIERSTEAD

Copyright © 2016 by Jenny Maria Kierstead
Published by Breathing Space Yoga under the imprint Yoga Books

All Rights Reserved. Except for use in any review, no part of this book may be reproduced, stored in a retrieval system, or transmitted in any form or by any means, electronic, mechanical, or otherwise, without written permission from the publisher.

Cover Image "She Lingers In The Dusty Rays" used with the kind permission of TJ Scott.
Cover Design and Interior Design by Woven Red Author Services, www.WovenRed.ca

Girl on Fire Empowerment Program/Jennifer Kierstead—1st edition
ISBN student manual paperback: 978-0-9953409-0-9
ISBN student manual ebook: 978-0-9953409-2-3

Contact Jenny at:
Jenny@GirlonFire.ca
www.YogaInSchools.ca
1 (902)-444-9642

Girl On Fire (Inferno Version)

Words and Music by Alicia Keys, Salaam Remi, Jeff Bhasker, Nicki Minaj and Billy Squier

Copyright (c) 2012 EMI April Music Inc., Lellow Productions, EMI Blackwood Music Inc., Linden Springfield, Sony/ATV Music Publishing LLC, Way Above Music, Money Mack Music, Harajuku Barbie Music and Songs Of The Knight

All Rights on behalf of EMI April Music Inc., Lellow Productions, EMI Blackwood Music Inc., Linden Springfield, Sony/ATV Music Publishing LLC and Way Above Music Administered by Sony/ATV Music Publishing LLC, 424 Church Street, Suite 1200, Nashville, TN 37219

All Rights on behalf of Money Mack Music and Harajuku Barbie Music Controlled and Administered by Songs Of Universal, Inc.

All Rights on behalf of Songs Of The Knight Controlled and Administered by Spirit Two Music, Inc.

International Copyright Secured All Rights Reserved

Reprinted by Permission of Hal Leonard Corporation

Dedication

The spark of this program was ignited when a local 17 year old girl took her life in 2013 after being victimized.

I, along with many others throughout Canada, was devastated by this outcome of violence inflicted on yet another young woman. At the news of her death, I went into deep reflection, asking how I could contribute by planting seeds of love and respect in the soil of her life's legacy. The following work is the answer to that question.

This program is dedicated to all the young women who, in the depths of a darkened reality, have taken their own lives. May we, in honour of their struggle, seize the invitation to show up fully in our lives and shine radiantly as Girls on Fire.

Table of Contents

WELCOME MESSAGE 13

WEEKLY PLAN 15

GIRL ON FIRE CODE OF CONDUCT 16

INTRODUCTION TO YOGA 17
    The balance of Hatha Yoga 17
    What is Yoga? 18
    The Effects of Yoga on the Nervous System 19
    A Note on Contemporary Yoga 20
    How to Approach the Movement Practice 21
    Preparing for Your First Class 21

WEEK 1 – WHAT IS THE "GIRL ON FIRE"? 24
    Let's Empower, Not Overpower 24
    10 Inner Treasures (Core Competencies) 24
    What does being healthy mean? 25
    What we know 25
    Stereotypes of Feminine and Masculine 26
        Feminine 26
        Masculine 27
    Girl on Fire Description 28
    A Message from Jenny 28
    Ritual 29
    What is Omwork? 30
    Mentor 30
    The Art of Affirmations or Mantras 30
        Sanskrit Mantras—Sacred Affirmations 30
        Your Core Mantra 31

    Guidelines for Creating Effective Affirmations 31
    Sample affirmations 32

Omwork 32
    Affirmation 33
    Physical Posture 33

Mindful Movement Class - Week 1 34
Notes 36

Week 2 – Self-Awareness 37

A Message from Jenny 37
Balance 38
Stream of Well-being 39
The Ayurvedic Approach to Health and Harmony 41
What is Ayurveda? 41
The 3 *Doshas* 41
    Vata/Air 42
    Pitta/Fire 43
    Kapha/Earth 44

Dysmorphophobia 45
Our changing brains 45
A Message from Jenny 46
Three Phases of Life 47
    Childhood 47
    Womanhood 48
    The Wise Woman 48

Change vs. Transformation 49
Omwork 49
    Self-acceptance and inner-beauty exercise 49
    Self-Love Quiz 50
    Lifelong Guide to Eating and Living.. 50
    Affirmation 51
    Physical Posture 51

Mindful Movement Class - Week 2 52
Notes 53

Week 3 – Self-Worth 54

The Ego 54
What we know 56
Self-Worth or Self-Esteem? 56
Chakras and The Fire Essence 57
    The most commonly known chakras 58

Fire Snuffing-factor—Shame 60
A Message from Jenny 60
Omwork 63
    Affirmations 64
    Physical Posture 64

Mindful Movement Class - Week 3 65
Notes 66

WEEK 4 – CONFIDENCE 67

Story of Swarupa, and our Girl on Fire Potential 67
Internally Referenced Living 68
A Message from Jenny 68
Bhoga versus Yoga 69
The Beauty Myth 70
    Self-punishment 71
    What does it mean to you to be a woman in the world today? 71

Cultivating Confidence 72
Girl on Fire Poem 73
Omwork 73
    Affirmation 74
    Physical Posture 74
    Additional Omwork Reading - Sleep 74

Mindful Movement Class - Week 4 77
Notes 78

WEEK 5 – DISCERNMENT 79

A Message from Jenny 79
Training the brain with BREATH 81
    Step 1: Breathe 81
    Step 2: Relax 82

    Step 3: Experience 82
    Step 4: Allow 82
    Step 5: Tend to the moment 82
    Step 6: Health 82
    Reflection 83

The Path of Behavior Change 83
    Phase 1: disorientation 83
    Phase 2: initial recognition 83
    Phase 3: familiar recognition 84
    Phase 4: avoidance 84
    Phase 5: a new path 84

Romance and rose colored glasses 84
Establishing healthy boundaries 85
Discussion time or inner reflection 87
Omwork 89
    A call to make a change 89
    Affirmations 90
    Physical posture 90
    Additional Omwork Reading 90

Mindful Movement Class - Week 5 92
Notes 93

WEEK 6 – RESILIENCE 94

Stoking the Fire 95
Soak in the *Sukha*, Distance the *Dukha* 95
Affirmation 96
A Message from Jenny 96
Healthy emotions 97
Pratipaksha Bhavana 98
    Admit 99
    Allow 99
    Act 100

Anxiety 101
Stress 102
Omwork 105
    Affirmations 106
    Physical Posture 106

Mindful Movement Class - Week 6 107
Notes 108

Week 7 – Discipline 109

A Message from Jenny 109
Developing Discipline 110
Technology and Social Media 112
Be your own vigilante 113
Boundaries and social media 113
What we know 114
The healing power of touch 114
Omwork 116
    Affirmations 116
    Physical posture 117

Mindful Movement Class - Week 7 118
Notes 120

Week 8 – Optimism 121

A Message from Jenny 121
Depression 122
Three types of depression 123
Yoga for depression 124
Why Optimism 124
The Body speaks your mind 125
Low and high power postures 126
The power of a smile 127
    Inner Smile 127

A call to make a change 128
Omwork 128
    Affirmations 129
    Physical posture 129

Mindful Movement Class - Week 8 130
Notes 131

Week 9 – Contentment 132

- A Message from Jenny 132
- Perfectionism vs Love 134
- Fixed versus Growth Mindset 134
- Seek wholeness, not perfection! 136
- Addiction 137
- Body Perfect 137
- Mistake of the Intellect 138
- Omwork 139
  - Affirmations 139
  - Physical posture 139
- Mindful Movement Class - Week 9 140
- Notes 142

Week 10 – Connection 143

- Kindness 143
- A Message from Jenny 145
- The Rainbow Story 145
- Conscious communication 147
- The Five A's 147
- Sisterhood Declaration 148
- Omwork 148
  - Affirmations 148
  - Physical Posture 148
- Mindful Movement Class - Week 10 149
- Notes 150

Week 11 – Essence 151

- A Message from Jenny 151
- I am Shakti 153
- Your Essence 153
- Pause for Reflection 154
- Your Life Purpose 155
- Conclusion 155
- Omwork 156
  - Affirmations 156

    Physical posture 156

  Mindful Movement Class - Week 11 157

  Notes 159

WEEK 12 – CELEBRATION 160

  Into the world with an unwavering sense of YOU! 160

  Time capsule Letter to the you in five years time 161

  A Message from Jenny 161

    Self-awareness 162

    Self worth 162

    Confidence 162

    Discernment 163

    Resiliency 163

    Discipline 163

    Optimism 163

    Contentment 163

    Connection 164

    Essence 164

  Notes 165

  Girl on Fire Reflection Questions 166

APPENDIX A – ABHYANGA INSTRUCTIONS 167

  Benefits of Abhyanga massage 167

  How to do Abhyanga 168

  Abhyanga and Yoga 168

APPENDIX B – REFERENCES AND RECOMMENDATIONS 169

APPENDIX C – RESOURCES 171

"Girl on Fire (Inferno Version)"
Alicia Keys, Salaam Remi, Jeff Bhasker, Nicki Minaj and Billy Squier

She's just a girl, and she's on fire
Hotter than a fantasy, lonely like a highway
She's living in a world, and it's on fire
Feeling the catastrophe, but she knows she can fly away

Oh, she got both feet on the ground
And she's burning it down
Oh, she got her head in the clouds
And she's not backing down

This girl is on fire
This girl is on fire
She's walking on fire
This girl is on fire

Looks like a girl, but she's a flame
So bright, she can burn your eyes
Better look the other way
You can try but you'll never forget her name
She's on top of the world
Hottest of the hottest girls say

Oh, we got our feet on the ground
And we're burning it down
Oh, got our head in the clouds
And we're not coming down

This girl is on fire
This girl is on fire
She's walking on fire
This girl is on fire

Everybody stands, as she goes by
Cause they can see the flame that's in her eyes
Watch her when she's lighting up the night
Nobody knows that she's a lonely girl
And it's a lonely world
But she gon' let it burn, baby, burn, baby

This girl is on fire
This girl is on fire
She's walking on fire
This girl is on fire

She's just a girl, and she's on fire

Welcome Message

Hello there, I'm glad you're here.

Do you struggle with the pressure to be someone other than yourself?

Do you feel overwhelmed by the thought of becoming an adult and everything that's involved with that role?

Do you sometimes feel alone, misunderstood and not recognized for what you are capable of?

If you answered yes to any of these questions then you're in the right place, and you're certainly not alone.

My name is Jenny Kierstead and I'm the founder of *Breathing Space Yoga Studios* and *Yoga in Schools*. While I currently live an amazing life filled with career success, relationship fulfilment and vibrant wellbeing, this wasn't always my reality. When I was 16 years old, my whole world came tumbling down around me—my dream of becoming a university basketball player was in jeopardy, my parents were divorcing, my dog who slept on my pillow each night was hit by a car and died, my boyfriend was diagnosed with cancer and my beloved grandmother passed away. While any one of these occurrences would be considered traumatic, I had all of them happen at once! It was indeed, the perfect storm.

Up until that point, my life had been status quo: the same house, same family structure, same routine and same friends. My parents were leaders in the community and very respected. My two siblings and I were well loved. People used to think of our family as the ideal. But behind our outwardly perfect image there was a storm stirring that would eventually crest into a massive wave of destruction.

And when it struck, I was completely ill-prepared. As I attempted to cling to the pieces of my crumbling world, I used what few coping mechanisms I had at the age of sixteen. I dealt with the perfect storm by controlling what aspects of life I could: my diet and my body. Before I realized what was actually happening, the dark power of anorexia took hold of my life and continued to do so for years.

After many years of suffering and many moments on the brink of giving up, I have emerged from the wreckage of that storm. I have also amassed incredible skills from years of cognitive therapy, bodywork, ancient healing practices, rigorous personal inquiry and service.

The teen years are the most creative, energetically charged years of our lives. My work over the last twenty years has been to create a repertoire of core competencies, or inner treasures as they are referred to here, to help those in this phase of life stay healthy and balanced.

Many people, like me, live through these years without effective life skills. For that reason, this program is truly applicable to women of all ages.

My hope is that this program will be deeply rewarding with content you will refer to for years to come. It is also my hope that this program ignites you and challenges you, calling you to reconsider habits that don't serve your highest potential. This work of questioning old ways of being requires great courage and faith on your behalf. Speaking from experience, you will not only survive, but come out on the other side thriving as a whole new version of yourself.

A Girl on Fire is a woman free to be who she was born to be, a woman who confidently shines her light essence into dark spaces and a woman with the power to wholeheartedly lead humanity into greater realms of consciousness, compassion and peace.

I hope this work transforms your life as much as it has mine.

May you be healed

May you be happy

May you know great joy

May you dwell in peace.

Weekly Plan

The Girl on Fire program consists of both theory and physical practice. There are elements of theory, group discussion and self-reflection as well as contemporary cognitive therapies and mindfulness practices drawn from various ancient healing traditions.

The class also includes a multidisciplinary movement practice designed to accommodate all levels of ability and experience. The movement practice is intended to help you integrate the classroom principles into your whole being, to release toxic stress chemicals, to learn simple tools for self-regulation, strengthen your body and reconnect with your body's signals and learn to listen to its messages. This will enhance your health, wellbeing and longevity.

Each weekly class is themed according to the 10 *Girl on Fire* inner treasures of self-awareness, self-worth, confidence, discernment, resilience, discipline, optimism, contentment, connection and essence. These inner treasures have been selected with the hope that by cultivating these core competencies, you will have the skills to live empowered, joy-filled, and harmonious lives.

Each week you will be sent home with reflective Omwork. The hope is that that you will apply these concepts in your daily personal lives. Omwork is a play on words, used to remind you of the meaning of Om, the great unifying vibration of all creation, and to clarify that your take-home material is not academic work, but rather deep, essential inner work. Often inner challenges seem insurmountable, but by incorporating these teachings into our daily lives one step at a time, using the power of ritual, we can make long term, life-altering changes.

Girl on Fire Code of Conduct

Confidentiality: In order to create a safe and supportive environment for all, I agree to respect the privacy of fellow participants by keeping what is shared within this program here.

Personal accountability: I realize that I may be emotionally triggered by some of the content or even by another participant, and I agree to be fully accountable for my actions.

Needs: I also agree to take responsibility for my needs, honoring them as they arise and asking for help when I need it. I understand that self-care is an inside job.

Conscious Communication: I agree to practise *ahimsa (kindness)* by communicating with fellow Girls on Fire with respect and inclusivity.

Bottom line: let's fuel each others fire, not snuff it out!

_____   _____
Name   Date

Introduction to Yoga

THE BALANCE OF HATHA YOGA

Each week we will be practicing Hatha yoga, or physical yoga. Hatha yoga works with the opposing solar (sun) and lunar (moon) energies in the body.

Just as our daily rhythm includes daytime, which is governed by the sun, and night-time, which is governed by the moon, we too are influenced by the same opposing energies within our bodies. At the core of ancient healing traditions there is a framework for the energy systems of our bodies, which are based on these opposite yet complementary energies of light and dark.

The physical practice of yoga, with its many variations, lies under the umbrella term of Hatha yoga, which comes from the language of yoga, called Sanskrit. Sanskrit is one of the oldest languages known to humankind and is very unique because it was created by yogic masters during heightened states of awareness. For this reason, Sanskrit terms often don't have an English equivalent as the words hold a vibrancy and an energetic potency that other languages just can't match.

According to the ancients, there are upwards of 80,000 channels of energy circulating through our bodies, with three main central channels. One channel resides on the right side of the spinal column, another on the left and the main one mimics the spinal column itself, running along the central nervous system; the spine and the brain.

The "Ha" in Hatha stands for the daytime aspect of our being, associated with the sun and its solar energy. This solar energy travels on the right side of the spine but its qualities are found throughout our body and mind. It suggests an inner luminosity or brightness, and relates to the quality of golden heat. It is action based and reflects courage, strength, steadfastness, fearlessness, confidence and willpower. Although it's not a gender reference (as men and women alike contain both energies), this solar energy is also referred to as masculine.

The "tha" in Hatha stands for the night-time aspect of our being, associated with the moon and its lunar energy. This lunar energy travels on the left side of the spine but its qualities are also found throughout our body and mind. It relates to the inward self-knowing awareness aspect of ourselves and holds the quality of silver coolness. Unlike its solar partner, tha is still, quiet, thought-driven, reflective, devotional, sensitive, wise, yielding, playful and compassionate. Again, this lunar energy is referred to as feminine in nature.

The Chinese symbol for light and dark, sun and moon, is the yin-yang symbol. It reflects the same theory that every living system contains opposing and complementary energies.

When the masculine and feminine energies within us, and around the world, are balanced and intertwined they give way to great harmony and creativity.

Nature is relentlessly searching for balance. At a cultural level, we are taught from an early age to be action based in our way of living: constantly on the go with little time for reflection and stillness. At a more global level, we currently see the results of the unconscious use of power (action based energy) when humans deforest the earth, contaminate the water and pollute the air we breathe. This is all causing devastating weather patterns as Mother Earth pushes back against these imbalances that have been created.

The world needs all of you to grow into adulthood with a sense of balance of both energies, and the awareness of your own brilliant light that is both powerful and compassionate, in order for the world to swing back into balance.

What is Yoga?

One of the most common definitions of yoga is that of union: the uniting of the body, mind, emotions and spirit. Yoga is the science of awakening our true essence, which lives in the deepest part of our being. Yogic philosophy outlines five layers that both conceal and contribute to our true nature.

The **outermost layer** is the one that people most easily relate to, the **physical body**. This translates from Sanskrit to English as the food sheath. The way in which we nourish ourselves not only with food and fluid, but also through movement, is reflected in our physical bodies. This program addresses the physical body with postures that are highly effective and yet simple enough for you to do on your own. What many find most interesting about postures is the remarkable improvements you may see in both strength and flexibility, a rare combination that few (if any) other forms of exercise offer.

The next layer is the **energy or vital body** which in yoga is called prana. For those who need to see things to believe them, this layer can be the topic of lively conversation. After a few yoga sessions, however, when one feels a vibration or pulse coursing through his/her limbs, there is no question that something beyond matter is animating our bodies. Through this practice, we learn to liberate and direct the natural flow of energy within our systems. The breathing practices in this program have been designed to awaken and refine our channels of energy, which can become blocked from stress and emotional disturbances.

There are many factors that influence our levels of energy. Some of the obvious ones are nutrition, sleep, exercise and stress. But we know there are more subtle factors that drain our energy, such as our thoughts. This leads us to the next layer which is a twofold construction involving the mind. One aspect of the **mind sheath is the intellect**, referring to our thoughts and judgments. It is here that we make choices about how we care for ourselves and what habits we choose to nurture. Stressful and anxious thoughts can be one of the greatest energy thieves and can lead to a cycle of obsessive thinking. Throughout this program, there are techniques for cultivating mental focus and discipline, which are necessary for turning off the negative inner dialogue and turning on the positive self-talk.

The next layer is the **wisdom or personality sheath**, where we experience intuition, insight and higher knowing. This unfolds naturally with a regular practice of yoga and meditation. At this point, we are beginning to explore the inner depths of our being, and move beyond the intellect. It is said that women naturally possess the gift of heightened sensitivity and intuition.

The **inner most layer** of our being is referred to as the **bliss layer or our true essence**. Our true essence, or the distinct light that we call you, is nurtured through our relationships with those around us and involves what most of us in the western world have limited comfort with--emotions. In yoga, emotions are approached as energy in motion or e-motion. They are not good or bad but rather a significant part of being alive.

No matter what difficulties you may be living with, inside all of us lies a sparkling jewel of beauty and creativity. Through asana (postures), deep breathing and meditation, we grow our ability to clear away the cobwebs, the blocks and the barriers, to access this hidden jewel within.

As we gain awareness of our own complexity and the various layers of our being, we can encourage our true nature to shine through in each action, breath, thought and emotion. The gifts of yoga extend beyond the physical benefits of increased strength, flexibility and balance. Through yoga, we learn to charge our energetic batteries, sharpen our mental focus and harness the power of our emotions. This allows us to ultimately rest in a state of being-ness where happiness, joy and peace flow with ease.

THE EFFECTS OF YOGA ON THE NERVOUS SYSTEM

Yoga serves people of every age, gender, race and ability. It creates lasting and positive change in a person's overall health. It enhances muscular strength throughout the body, increases flexibility, facilitates weight loss and stimulates immunity as well as the efficiency of our vital organs.

Beyond the physical benefits, yoga works on more subtle levels to calm our worried minds and focus our scattered thoughts, allowing for a deep letting go within our core.

The generalized feeling of calm and resilience that comes from doing yoga stems from the regulation of one of the most important systems of the body: the nervous system. The nervous system is a vital structure that influences the essential functions of the body/mind; from our digestive organs to our locomotive system to brain activity.

The **central nervous system**, housed within the spinal cord, is said to be the main communicator, transmitting messages from the brain to the body and vice versa. Neurotransmitters tell the brain what is happening in the body. This system gives instructions to all parts of the body in every waking moment.

The **peripheral nervous system** is comprised of the **sympathetic** and **parasympathetic** systems. The sympathetic system is designed to protect us from danger by triggering the flight, fight or freeze reaction. When we encounter a threat, or a perceived threat, which may be a busy hallway during a break or a fire alarm, the system produces stress hormones to give us the extra energy to conquer the threat. When the sympathetic nervous system is activated, the following physiological changes occur:

- Release of adrenaline and other stress hormones
- Increased heart rate
- Increased blood pressure
- Increased oxygen consumption
- Increased carbon dioxide expulsion
- Rapid, shallow breathing
- Profuse sweating
- Decreased growth hormone production
- Suppression of immune system

In the wake of a stressful encounter, the body's natural inclination is to slow down, rest and recover. This natural recovery phase often isn't factored into our daily schedules, and as we rush from one stressful event to another, the damaging effects of stress accumulate. The **parasympathetic nervous system** is known as the "rest and relaxation" aspect of our system. This system is awakened during meditation, conscious breathing and yoga, especially at the end of a yoga class in Savasana, or relaxation pose. When this system is aroused, the following physiological changes occur:

- Heart rate slows down
- Blood pressure normalizes
- Oxygen use diminishes
- Breathing slows
- Immune function improves

Nischala Joy Devi in her book *The Healing Path of Yoga* says, "I find it quite interesting that, with all the many wonderful and important things we learn in school, relaxation is stunted at our kindergarten graduation."[1]

A healthy nervous system is what enables us to maintain composure during stressful times. Yoga nurtures the cells of our nervous system by cleansing away stress hormones while fueling our cells with oxygen and energy. Yoga also trains the system to be mindfully alert and responsive, instead of impulsive and overly reactive.

Despite its long list of physical benefits, yoga can profoundly enhance our lives off the mat. By re-establishing our sense of inner balance and wellbeing, yoga is a wonderful partner on the path of becoming who we really want to be. This work will help you to clarify how you want to live, how you want to contribute to the world and exactly how you want to feel while you're doing it all.

Being a Girl on Fire will help you step into this vision!

A Note on Contemporary Yoga

In some forms of yoga, sexuality is considered a distraction from the path. Therefore, strong asana practices were prescribed to help restrain one's sexual impulses. Other forms of yoga bring sexuality into the teachings, working with sexual energy as a way of charging one's practice. In both approaches however, the goal is to harness this highly creative energy in

---

[1] Nischala Joy Devi, The Healing Path of Yoga (Harmony June 6, 2000), 67.

order to use it for purposes of personal growth, creative expression and positive contribution. In the adolescent phase of life, sexual energy is very strong and yet the maturity to manage it effectively so is not yet developed; so learning to channel it is a worthy practice.

Today, there are misguided female leaders of 'yoga' who are using their sex appeal to gain YouTube popularity and while they may be successful at doing that, they have veered from the path of yoga. A woman moving with poise, strength and grace is indeed an attractive sight to witness and something to aspire toward. But as modern yoginis, you are NOT expected to display your body in suggestive positions while wearing a bikini. Including yoga in the context of erotica is not only an inaccurate demonstration of the practice, but a violation of our collective aspirations to transcend sexual objectification and to be viewed as respected, capable, intelligent women of worth.

How to Approach the Movement Practice

The goal of our movement practice is to anchor our awareness in our bodies and our breath, moment by moment. As we do that, we familiarize ourselves with sensations and the messages within them. The more listening we do, the more healing we do, and whenever there's healing, there's freedom and happiness.

In the western world, we have stuffed the wisdom tradition of yoga into the same box as our beauty obsessed, consumer driven paradigm, as we associate yoga with other 'body sculpting' exercises. The true practice of yoga and other ancient energy management techniques call us to use these tools to expand our consciousness beyond our neurotic, contracted ego perspective into an awareness of the interconnectedness of life.

If you have thought that you are not fit, firm or toned enough to try yoga, you have been misinformed of the true purpose and intent of the practice. You need not change a thing about yourself before you embark on the journey. Instead, the best way to prepare starts by accepting the invitation to show up on your mat with full acceptance of you who you are now, and a commitment to deepening your understanding, and compassion for yourself, for others and for life.

Preparing for Your First Class

What do I bring?

Yoga mat
Water bottle
Journal (optional)

What do I wear?

Comfortable clothing, like sweats or leggings that allow you to move freely, but not so loose that clothing impedes movement.

What can I expect?

Each class will begin with a visualization or a mindfulness practice with breath awareness in an easy sitting pose or lying down pose. Following this opening segment will be warming postures that increase circulation and prepare your body for more challenging (optional) poses that flush toxins and ignite your healing flame. The class will culminate with a cooling or relaxation phase, designed to help you integrate your experience and insights before heading back into your life.

Each class includes ancient healing techniques and postures, mindfulness practices, partner yoga opportunities as well as quiet reflection.

Ritual on your mat

It is recommended that you take this time on your mat to enjoy solitude while doing your own postures to help you become more self aware and to engage the partner or group activities in a way that honors your own comfort level. Your facilitator may come around to enhance your practice with physical assists, moving your body in subtle ways to promote greater alignment, which you can choose to accept or not.

To assist you in honoring your growing edge during your practice, each participant will choose a sign that either indicates permission for the facilitator to assist you, or declines the offering. This is your freedom to choose one way or the other, in each given practice, and the instructor will not take your choice personally.

Finally, as your movement class comes to a close, it is recommended to wipe down your mat, not only as a courtesy for the next class, but also as a symbolic gesture of wiping your slate clean after releasing aspects of your past that don't serve you today.

What do you know about yoga?

Many people today do yoga as a form of exercise to tighten and tone and sweat away pounds. While it may do all of those things, the practice is designed to both push your physical edge with an element of challenge AND create a sense of relaxed, focused awareness.

In each movement class we do, your challenge will be to find that sweet spot in between effort and ease, which we'll call your growing edge. If you practice beneath your edge by not giving enough physically, or by drifting your attention away from the experience, no change will result. If you overdo it and work too hard, you'll exhaust yourself and risk injury.

When we practice breathing and moving within the boundaries of our growing edge, we fuel our fire and boost our energy. You know you're on track when you naturally look and feel more alive, healthy, centered and peaceful, and people start asking what you're doing differently.

Here are a few signs of a successful, self honoring practice

You have: strong digestion, a clear tongue, a pleasant fragrance to the body, a good complexion, easy and regular elimination, a feeling of lightness, a feeling of flexibility and resilience, mental clarity and calm.

Counter that list with these signs of an improper, or ego driven practice

You experience: pain, tension, injury, severe fatigue, soreness, nausea, indigestion, anxiety, irritability, dullness and congestion.

Ready Girls on Fire? Let do this!

Week 1 – What is the "Girl on Fire"?

This week's focus is to gain a deeper understanding of:
- Welcome and overview of the program
- 10 Inner treasures
- Feminine and masculine stereotypes
- What is a Girl on Fire?

LET'S EMPOWER, NOT OVERPOWER

The intention of this program is to empower you as a young woman and to recognize the strength of your feminine energy in a way that respects, not diminishes, the masculine. We are shifting from the oppression of women into a reality of equality. We are not claiming to be better than guys, but rather members of the same human race with gifts of equal value.

Did you know that in many workplaces, women are still paid less than men for the same job?

As the pendulum swings back into balance between the sexes, the shift is creating some waves. Some men feel threatened by women who stand in their strength and effectively assume roles they've never claimed before. But we are not attempting to overpower or horde all the opportunities. This is not about striving for superiority or control over anyone. It is simply about **a readiness to walk side-by-side, with mutual respect for what we as women have to offer.** When we feel valued and appreciated, we shine our brightest light. And when women shine fully, the whole world alights with kindness, creativity and caring.

10 INNER TREASURES (CORE COMPETENCIES)

Each weekly class is themed according to the 10 Girl on Fire inner treasures. These inner treasures have been selected with the hope that by cultivating these core competencies, you will have the skills to live empowered, joy-filled, and harmonious lives.
1) Self-awareness
2) Self-worth
3) Confidence
4) Discernment
5) Resilience

6) Discipline
7) Optimism
8) Contentment
9) Connection
10) Essence

What does being healthy mean?

In yoga, health, or *svasthi*, is defined as a woman who is well-established in herself. She is the strong, confident, balanced woman who exudes the qualities of good health that most of us would describe as well-nourished, joyful, radiant, warm and enthusiastic.

Instead of looking outside of yourself for answers to life's questions, you are invited throughout this program to look inside for the answers to your deepest questions. By tapping into your own innate intelligence, you will access the ability to maintain your own vibrant health and facilitate your own self-healing. Instead of relying on an expert to fix your problems—which we are taught to do in this culture—you will be encouraged to pay attention to your very own inner healer. By listening to your own needs and applying these simple and easy techniques, you will become the expert of your own life. As a Girl on Fire, you will learn to become self-established and self-reliant, balanced in body, mind, and emotions.

As human beings, our highest state is having the awareness that we are interconnected and actually one with all that is. This includes the many multidimensional aspects of ourselves (body, energy, mind, wisdom and our true nature), as well as our immediate surroundings (community) and our extended environment (the entire universe). In a state of oneness—or unity—we literally *become* the world and experience the infinite power and presence of all that is.

In Western culture—with our obsession with external pursuits, technology, material consumption, physical perfection and money—we have become dangerously disconnected from the needs of the natural environment, and from our own needs.

This Girl on Fire program is designed to help you remember who you are by bringing parts of yourself back together as a whole. That means re-integrating your mind, your body and your soul. When this happens, you will become grounded, strong and centered in who you are as a radiant young woman with a specific and wonderful purpose. When challenge strikes in your future, which it will, it is our intention to have provided you with the inner resources to skillfully navigate your way through it, or at least, the awareness to seek assistance from a trusted source.

What we know

- Approximately 91% of women are unhappy with their bodies and resort to dieting to achieve their ideal body shape. Unfortunately, only 5% of women naturally possess the body type often portrayed by Americans in the media.[2]

---

[2] "11 Facts About Body Image", Do Something.org, accessed September 2016, https://www.dosomething.org/facts/11-facts-about-body-image

- Women are still significantly underpaid in the work-force. Even working full-time, women continue to bring home 20% less than the men that work beside them. That includes women with university degrees. Aboriginal women, radicalized women and immigrant women take home even less.[3]
- Plastic surgeries are now up into the millions per year. Girls will go to great lengths to try and achieve the perfect body. In just one year, the number of girls aged 18 and younger who had breast implants nearly tripled.[4]
- In the United States, 20 million women and 10 million men suffer from a clinically significant eating disorder at some time in their life.[5]
- Some of the top mental health challenges among 8 to 15-year-olds are ADHD, mood or depressive disorders, anxiety, and eating disorders.[6]

Stereotypes of Feminine and Masculine

Feminine

What is feminine? Media claims that feminine is sexy, passive, pretty, external, skinny.

Does this woman look happy? Empowered? Feminine?

Most runway models meet the body mass index physical criteria for anorexia.

Twenty years ago, the average fashion model weighed 8% less than the average woman. Today she weighs 23% less.[7]

These bizarrely unfeminine beauty standards have actually made women look like skinny, unhappy bags of bones. Society has disempowered and starved the feminine, draining us of our life force, which flows when we live within a healthy body weight.

True femininity expresses itself in all shapes, sizes and colors.

Feminine energy is graceful, fluid, watery, creative, wild, round, full, assertive, bold, sensual, healing, still, dark, incubating, nurturing, reflective, intuitive, compassionate, all-embracing, listening.

---

[3] "The Best and Worst Places to be a Woman in Canada 2015", Canadian Centre for Policy Alternatives, accessed September 2016, https://www.policyalternatives.ca/sites/default/files/uploads/publications/National%20Office/2015/07/Best_and_Worst_Places_to_Be_a_Woman2015.pdf

[4] "The Facts about Girls in Canada", Canadian Women's Foundation, accessed September 2016, http://www.canadianwomen.org/facts-about-girls

[5] "Get the Facts on Eating Disorders", NEDA Feeding Hope, accessed September 2016, https://www.nationaleatingdisorders.org/get-facts-eating-disorders

[6] "Any Disorder Among Children", National Institute of Mental Health, accessed September 2016, https://www.nimh.nih.gov/health/statistics/prevalence/any-disorder-among-children.shtml

[7] "Plus Sized Bodies, What's wrong with them Anyway?", Plus Model, accessed September 2016, http://www.plus-model-mag.com/2012/01/plus-size-bodies-what-is-wrong-with-them-anyway/

How do these images differ from the ones we see in the media today?

Traditionally, women and Goddesses had robust, curvy, full figures. They were nurturing and life sustaining, like the sacred cow in India that is so highly revered for her ability to sustain life with her milk. In fact, the cow is such a highly honored symbol of sustenance that even McDonald's doesn't serve beef in India.

Women naturally have higher levels of adipose/fat tissue than men so that we can nourish our families and live a long, healthy life. In some cultures today, a larger figure is symbolic of prosperity, reflecting enough financial means to abundantly provide for our needs.

Today, however, we have become fat phobic and many women have developed obsessions with fat, spending their whole lives battling the bulge and moving from one diet to another. There is even a medical term for it, called body image distortion—or dysmorphophobia.

In order for women to heal our broken relationships with our bodies, we must take on the challenge of breaking out of the current feminine belief structure that society has created for us. If we are honest with ourselves, it becomes apparent that our true purpose is not to achieve physical perfection in order to meet the passing beauty standards of our time. Nor is it our sole purpose to be the vehicles of sexual satisfaction for men.

While it's important to feel good about our bodies and our sexuality, could there be a higher calling for us?

In the yoga tradition, feminine energy is called *Shakti*. It is the creative force of the universe that resides within the body, specifically at the base of the spine. Through mindfulness and yoga practices, it actively moves up the central channels along the spinal column, clearing blockages, healing illnesses, awakening our energy and expanding our awareness.

Shakti is a powerful force of feminine energy. It is the primal creative principle underlying the cosmos and the energizing essence of embodied spirit. According to the ancient yogis, the whole universe is the manifestation of Shakti.

Shakti is also known as *devi*, from the root div "to shine" so we could say she is "the shining one." In the *Rig Veda*, one of the oldest Indian spiritual texts on yoga, Aditi is the goddess of the great womb, the mother of the entire universe, and holds *agni*, the essence of fire, in her womb, much like a mother does with a baby.

Aditi is shining and luminous. She upholds the law and enforces justice. She is closely identified with the cow. As legend has it, the milk pours down from the cosmic cow, providing daily nourishment and life substance to all that is.

We can see that femininity is the female generative force that is both nourishing, like the cow, as well as luminous, shining and igniting like the fire essence.

Masculine

What is the masculine stereotype that is portrayed in society today?

Often we think of it as power hungry, aggressive, controlling, hard, tough, all-knowing, emotionless. This is NOT a true depiction of masculine energy, but a reflection of an imbalanced state.

In yoga, Shiva is the masculine energy that resides at the top of the spine as pure potential, awaiting the rise of its counterpart, Skakti. Shiva is the being while Shakti is the becoming. Shiva without Shakti is powerless and Shakti without Shiva is without purpose. We can see then, just how crucial it is to respect both energies of the feminine and masculine within all of us, women and men alike, since an imbalance of either one causes ill health.

Girl on Fire Description

In yoga there are two concepts: (prakasha) "luminosity" and (vimarsha) "mirror."

Luminosity is the light of lights, the source of all light, which we will discover within ourselves through this program.

The mirror is the reflection of this eternal light. Without it, the light of all lights would never be seen. It is one thing to shine our light when we are alone, but it's most important that we shine our light out for others to receive and be nourished by. We are not here to shine privately, we are here to unearth our gifts, and use them to contribute positively to the unfolding of the universe. The source light of the universe shines through us as radiant light and love, not to be kept hidden, but to be shared with and mirrored back by those around us. Our light illuminates others lives and vice versa.

In order to keep our inner light well lit, we need to keep our inner flame at our core well stoked. Over the course of this program, we'll talk about things that dampen our flame, which we'll call fire snuffers, and how we can protect our fire from these draining sources. We'll also discuss the many ways that we can nurture our flame to keep the bonfire within glowing brightly. This, we will call fire fuel.

A Message from Jenny

Throughout this program I have added excerpts from my memoir in progress about my struggle, my awakening and my eventual triumph over anorexia and how I've emerged from my severely imbalanced state to a life of true joy.

When the Dalai Lama was asked how to build self-esteem, it took three translators to explain the concept. He had never heard of poor self-esteem and never experienced it within his spiritually rich, community-based Tibetan culture.

When I was young, I experienced the worst poverty in life: a lack of respect and esteem for myself. I was like a baby bird with defective wings, and when it came time to fly, I flopped instead. Only after much suffering and searching, would I eventually gain faith in my own wings and discover the necessary tools to fly freely.

After many years of deep inner work and personal growth, I now live with strong and capable wings, giving myself permission to express my gifts through my work. I am challenged and rewarded daily in my role as parent of two amazing Girls on Fire in the making, and my intimate relationship with my husband is grounded in love, trust, transparency and humor.

In the beginning, a seed only needs an itty bitty ounce of nourishment to grow. This nourishment may come in the form of curiosity, or hope, or even despair. It doesn't matter what fuels your journey, so long as you take it. Have patience and relax your expectations of yourself. My advice for you at the beginning of this powerful journey is to simply be willing. Be willing to learn new skills, to leave the past behind you and courageously step into the new territory of your authentic, brilliant self.

Healing can be slow and mucky, but it can also be instantaneous as well. You may find that one week of practice suddenly opens you to a new way of thinking, altering your world forever, and for the better. I've learned throughout my journey of healing that anything is possible when we open our hearts. Let yourself be surprised and delighted and know that I am your greatest cheerleader on this brave and rewarding path.

Jenny

Ritual

The beautiful thing about becoming more mindful and self-aware, is realizing that we have the power to choose our inner attitude. Once we understand that feeling bad (and the complaining that goes along with it) is optional, we can then decide how we want to feel. What is your ideal feeling state? This program is designed to help you choose feeling good over feeling negative for the rest of your life.

Once you have a sense of how you want to feel inside, you can selectively identify things in your environment that support your new attitude. Did you know that you're allowed to leave a party, or walk out of a movie theatre, or ask your dentist to turn off frightening news on the TV or request a change in gossipy conversation if these things don't align with your intentions?

One of the most powerful ways we can bring ourselves back to wholeness and our desired feeling state is to practice the simple art of ritual. Ritual is the act of doing something with the intention of connecting with our highest and brightest self within a safe environment. Rituals help us to release old, outmoded habits, and invoke ways of being that are more aligned with our true self and the pure desires of the heart.

Incorporating ritual into your daily life affirms your desire to become an empowered, strong young woman with a secure sense of self-worth. You are invited to create a special place and time in your life for the self-reflective work you will be doing throughout this program. Whether it's a corner table in your bedroom or a whole room designed to reflect your highest vision, work with what you have. Frame inspiring images and choose symbolic items like stones, shells and candles that help to anchor you in feelings of goodness and remind you of your dreams.

The mind and body respond well to consistency, so set aside the same time in the same place each day to do this juicy work of reciting affirmations, sitting in silence, aligning with a person of success, reviewing Girl on Fire notes, writing, singing, you name it. Your future is worthy of this time, even if it's just five or ten minutes each day.

What is Omwork?

Om is a sacred symbol of unity, oneness with ourselves, others and the creative force of the Universe. It is known to be akin to the most basic primordial sound of the Universe. Reciting Om is said to invoke a sense of peace, unity consciousness and love.

Each week, you will be sent home with reflective "Omwork", with the hopes that you will apply these concepts in your daily personal life. Omwork is a play on words, used to remind you of the meaning of Om, the great unifying vibration of all creation. It is also used to clarify that your take home material is not academic work, but rather, the deep, essential inner work of the self. Often inner challenges seem insurmountable but by incorporating these teachings into your daily lives one step at a time, you can make long term, life altering changes.

Your Omwork will also include affirmations or statements that you can repeat to yourself on a daily basis. You can use our suggested affirmations each day, or create your own!

Mentor

This week, choose a female mentor who you look up to, but who is not a family member. You might want to pick a neighbor or a community member. Every two weeks or so, meet with your mentor to discuss your progress with the program and your life goals. You could also use this time as an opportunity to learn more about your mentor's passions, skills and dreams.

The Art of Affirmations or Mantras

The electromagnetic power of the heart is 5,000 times more powerful than the mind.

When manifesting change in our lives, we must enlist the power of the heart's field, making statements (or affirmations) that align with our passions and interests.

Affirmations are positive, affirming statements that express our desired path.

Mantras come from the ancient language of Sanskrit, and align us with the sacred energies of the Universe.

Sanskrit Mantras—Sacred Affirmations

The word Sanskrit comes from "Sanskrita" which means "well put together" because it was meticulously formed by highly awakened yogis. Sanskrit, therefore, is known to hold great power and can transmit rich spiritual energy. Unlike English and other languages, Sanskrit helps us to move beyond everyday thinking, to explore greater spiritual realities.

The vibration of sanskrit mantras, spoken through the human voice, are related to the energy centers within our bodies, called chakras. Let your mantra be a source of comfort and inspiration for you, so choose one that engenders feelings of goodness and comfort.

Your Core Mantra

Core mantras were traditionally given to a yoga practitioner from her teacher; however, we can choose our own based on how it resonates with us. The core mantra serves to remind us of our innermost self, aligning us with our unchanging, powerful, beautiful and awe-inspiring soul-force. The simplest core mantra available to us is OM, the sound of all Creation, symbolic of the energy of the Universe that unifies all things and all beings. The following mantra could also stand as your core mantra that you can recite anytime to re-establish your attention on your inner core power and your stream of well-being, as a Girl on Fire.

Sample of a Core mantra: I have faith, or I trust, or I am peace, or I am grateful, or I embody joy, or I am light.

Is there a word or brief phrase that comes to your mind that reflects your unique true nature?

Guidelines for Creating Effective Affirmations

- **Purge the old:** begin by acknowledging that your negative self-talk must be eliminated. We need to let go of the old ways first, in order to welcome the new.
- **Make it personal**: you cannot change anyone else's beliefs, attitudes or habits but your own! Write it in your own language, it must feel comfortable to say.
- State it in the **present moment**: not "I will be so excited " but rather "I am so excited that..."
- **Make it positive!**
- **Be Precise**: avoid wishful statements such as "I would love to have a car one day " and say instead "I love my new vehicle." Use present tense language, as we are inviting our dream into reality. Being specific is also key.
- **Include emotion:** describing strong emotional states will attract your intentions to you much quicker. Use highly charged emotional words, such as adjectives like: fantastic, exhilarating, outstanding, stunning, thrilling or exciting. And adverbs such as passionately, lovingly or joyfully.
- **Create statements that jazz you up.** Your new thoughts need to offer a sense of hope, excitement and motivation for the future. They need to inspire you to take action.
- **KISS: keep it simple sister**
- **Make it possible**
- Finish with the **desired result,** (avoid stating the problem): "I am happily working at my job as a life guard." Feel the feeling of arriving there now.
- **Persist until you succeed and repetition works**!
- **Update your affirmations** as you refine intentions and as you achieve your goals.
- Finally, you will transform your existing limitations into a new reality of strength, freedom, courage and confidence!

Sample affirmations

I feel amazing as I grow stronger and more confident in who I am everyday!
Today, I totally and completely love and accept myself, just as I am.
Today, I look in the mirror and love myself.
I am happily enjoying my new loving and supportive relationship/friendships.
I relax knowing that the world is filled with goodness.
I attract only love into my life.
I am everything that I choose to be. I am as unlimited as the endless universe.
I let go and trust the process.

Omwork

Complete the Ayurvedic questionnaire and read through the protocol on your specific body/mind type.

Set your alarm to go off ten minutes earlier each morning this week and take the extra time to lie in bed and simply reflect. Notice any negative self talk you are met with, and remember your affirmation work. Have a journal or iPad nearby to take notes on your mental ramblings while still in the open, peaceful, theta mind state.

The first few mornings, take time to reflect on the woman you are longing to become. Identify a woman whom you know or know of, who embodies your highest vision of what it means to be fully female. Record the attributes of this woman that you admire and strive to possess yourself.

As your list becomes more and more clear, spend the next few mornings imagining yourself assuming the same admirable traits. Let your imagination lead this exercise and let your conscious mind follow the vision. What do you, as a future Girl on Fire, look like? Include your hairstyle, your fashion style, your posture and your facial expression? Chances are you will have some challenges imagining your future self showing up fully in her life, because if you had no challenges around this conversation, you'd already be her.

Spend the next few mornings journaling about the blocks in the way—what is stopping you from dreaming up this vision of your future self? You're invited to do a free write (meaning that you forget about grammar and sentence structure and just let your thoughts flow onto the page) about any fears, doubts or denial you have around giving yourself permission to shine. Whatever is in the way, write it down and describe it in as much detail as you can. Reread what you wrote in your free write. Can you see why you have created this block in your life? Can you see how it protects you but also diminishes your flame? If you can, share it with a trusted friend, family member or facilitator.

Finally, instead of attempting to push through the wall of resistance with willpower—which most of us are taught to do in this driven, type-A society—try just being with the resistance compassionately. Imagine how you'd be with a friend who's struggling to overcome her own resistance and give yourself the same space. We're not giving into the resistance and letting it rule our lives, nor are we withdrawing or ignoring this roadblock. We are acknowledging it and naming the white elephant in the room: the issue that you know is there but have chosen to avoid up until now. Simply allow it to just be there, as you learn to foster self awareness. You may even spend some time communicating with this part of yourself that is standing in the way of you becoming a Girl on Fire. Does this wall of resistance have a specific name or title? It might be inner doubt, unworthiness or fear.

What purpose is this block serving? Perhaps it was established to keep you safe and protected, but it has also likely kept you from taking risks and living life fully.

Can you imagine replacing this resistance with a more empowering, liberating mechanism, like acting in a way that moves you closer to your vision?

Affirmation

True femininity expresses itself in all shapes, sizes and colors.

I have one body and only one body. It is the vehicle that will take me through the rest of my life.

I am light.

I make wise and healthy choices that support my overall wellbeing.

Personal additions:

Commit your affirmation to memory and post it in visible places.

Place an image on your alter or designated reflection space of an inspiring Girl on Fire whose flame is glowing brightly, with a list of her character traits that you aspire to have.

Physical Posture

Seated Jelly Fish

Mindful Movement Class - Week 1

NOTE: This is the Mindful Movement Class to accompany Week 1. For consistency and ease, we recommend the video series of these classes available at www.GirlOnFire.ca.

Weekly theme – What is a girl on Fire?
Sukhasana/Easy Pose **Feature Posture**: Seated Jelly Fish Seated Side Stretch Table Top with Knee to Nose flow Plankasana Cobra to Child's Pose Vinyasa Downward Dog Low Lunge Twisting Lunge Standing Rag Doll Mountain Pose Warrior 1 to Bowing Warrior 1 Table Top Basic Side Plank on hand and knee Cobra 3x **Partner Posture:** Lizard on a rock Seated Forward Bend Savasana/Relaxation Pose
Reflection Gayatri Chant - Gayatri is reflective of the female creative energy of the Universe. It is one of yoga's most sacred mantras, which is a phrase spoken in the ancient language of Sanskrit. Used in important rites of passage, representing intelligence and spiritual radiance, the Gayatri is an ideal mantra for the Girl on Fire journey. If however, you are not drawn to this mantra, please choose your own affirmative statement to recite at the beginning or closing of your practice session, or in other moments of quiet reflection. The chant to the Spirit within the fire, the Gayatri Mantra purifies the chanter and uplifts the listener. But for ages, this chant was a well-guarded secret, withheld from women who were relegated to the rolls of caretaker and householder. Today, however, it is sung by many around the world, including women, with reverence and love. Because it is an earnest and heartfelt invocation for awakening, it can be universally applied to all traditions. It really doesn't matter what your religion, your color or your ethnicity is – what matters is your intent and your willingness to heal and grow. It is said that the Gayatri spirals

from the heart of the chanter throughout the entire Universe, as we invoke peace and wisdom for all.

"May the Divine Light of the Universe illuminate us and lead us along the path of awakening".

Oṃ bhūr bhuvaḥ svaḥ
tát savitúr váreṇ(i)yaṃ
bhárgo devásya dhīmahi
dhíyo yó naḥ pracodáyāt

As you chant, you can envision yourself unfolding in ever widening rings of lotus petals, expanding into the fullest version of you.

Girl on Fire closing

To acknowledge the three centers of Power, Love and Insight:

Rise to sitting and bring palms together. Lift hands so that thumbs touch the mid eye point and say: *"Guided by insight"*

Now draw hands to heart, one palm on heart center in the middle of the chest and the other palm resting on top of the first hand and say: *"I listen to my heart's desire"*

Now take the top hand and slide it down so it rests on the navel, with the first hand remaining on the heart and say: *"And take positive, powerful action in the world"*

Notes

Week 2 – Self-Awareness

This week's focus is to gain deeper understanding of:
- The inner competency of self-awareness
- The stream of well-being and finding our balance
- Ayurveda and keeping your dosha in balance

A Message from Jenny

During my final year of high school, after basketball season was over, I decided I would play around with dieting for a few weeks. After all, according to my weight watchers consultation, I had an extra 10 lbs I was carrying around (I was at a perfect weight for an athletic 16-year-old, but they were in the business of weight loss).

What began as an innocent decrease of calories during a very stressful time in my life, exploded into a colossal loss of thirty pounds within a few months. At a time when my life was crashing down all around me, I had found something I could actually control, and it was the only source of power I could grasp. My parents were pre-occupied with their own painful divorce, and my health continued to dramatically spiral outside of the stream of well-being.

Mom had to call my sister to warn her of my condition before she returned home from an exchange in France. I recall hearing her crying on the phone informing Lisa that "She's just stopped eating. Some days we only see her eat an apple and rice cakes." By the time September came around, my dream of playing university basketball was completely in jeopardy. At the first practice for the Acadia women's team, the top rookie recruit was being tossed around on the court like a feather in the wind. This was not only my first practice, but my last.

If only I'd had the self awareness that I was off track and hurting, I could have reached out for proper help before it escalated into a full-blown eating disorder which claimed six years of my life.

I often reflect on my journey of recovery from exercise addiction and anorexia, and recently I asked myself if I could narrow it down to one thing that helped the most, what would it be? My answer continues to be self-awareness and self-inquiry. This unique faculty we have to witness ourselves in time and space is known today as mindfulness.

By inquiring into the reasons why we live the way we do, many answers to our suffering surface. This personal inquiry also calls us to take full responsibility for the state of our lives today. As children we are most certainly at the mercy of life's circumstances and have little control of our own lives. But as JK Rowling said in her address to Harvard graduates, "When we become adults, there is an expiry date on blaming our parents for the troubles we have."

I spent many years blaming others for my predicament, eventually coming to the conclusion that blame is the lowest form of problem solving. What's the most effective form of problem solving? Non-judgmental, compassionate self-awareness. The more we learn about how we got ourselves into a state of being, the sooner we can heal and move on to brighter skies.

As we venture through this program, it is my hope that you will sharpen your ability to observe yourself in a variety of different situations; noticing how you are with the silence of being by yourself, noting what triggers strong emotion and reactions in you, noticing when you feel the impulse to self-harm, or to lash out at others. All of it. The practice of self-awareness is almost like dating yourself. By slowly familiarizing yourself with the landscape of your inner life, you can more skillfully identify a) what needs you have and b) how to fulfill them in a healthy fashion.

For me, self-awareness led me to understand the factors involved in my illness, and that understanding led to the solution, which entailed patching up the hole in my bucket of self-worth so that I could receive love and nourishment.

You can only make positive changes in your life by becoming aware of the way in which you're living right now. No matter what it is, whether it's your breathing, your diet or your thoughts, everything changes for the better when we put it under the light of conscious awareness with a sense of curiosity and compassion. Self-awareness might possibly be the most important virtue you ever cultivate in your life, and one you can spend your whole life developing. Because of its significance to our personal growth, self-awareness is an inner treasure that will be practiced throughout the whole program.

Balance

> There is no possibility of one becoming a yogi if one eats too much, or eats too little, sleeps too much or does not sleep enough. She who is moderate in her habits of eating, sleeping, working and recreation can relieve the pains of this world by practicing the yoga system. ~ Bhagavad Gita, Chapter 6, verse 16-17

The concept of balance is a personal, unique measurement that's contingent on your temperament and tendencies. Running 10km a day may seem totally crazy for one person but may feel like good medicine for another. Working only 4 hours a day may appear lazy to one person, but this may be the ideal amount for another person to manage in order to maintain wellness.

In our overworked, non-stop society we may see balance as boring and somehow related to mediocrity.

In reality, living an imbalanced life demands more of us than we are able to keep up with. This can cause chronic stress, leading to a constant state of fight, flight or freeze. This causes ill-health, fatigue and a host of stress-related issues, including early aging.

We'll talk more about stress later in the program.

On the other hand, high levels of creativity, sparks of inspiration and spontaneous bouts of joy are all signs of a life in balance. That's our goal as a Girl on Fire.

STREAM OF WELL-BEING

This diagram of the stream of well-being indicates that our most natural state of being is one of health and vitality. When we live within these bounds of the stream of well-being, we live with balance, harmony, ease and resiliency. According to most ancient systems of natural medicine, the main channels of energy that sustain life travel within this stream. There are two lines of energy that start at each nostril and flow over the head and down the spine to the tailbone. The main and most powerful channel mimics the spinal column, traveling along the mid line of the body from crown to tailbone. When this central channel is open and free flowing, we experience well being, when it is blocked, like a kink in our hose, we experience impaired health. Our work then is to strive to keep these channels open and our energy focused on living within this literal and metaphorical stream of well-being. When we veer outside of this stream of well-being and balanced living, we experience health challenges, un-ease and eventually disease.

In the ancient model of Ayurvedic medicine, there are actually seven stages to illness. The first stage is the initial, subtle sign of disharmony, such as fatigue or a specific ache, and the final stage expresses itself as advanced illness or disease. Most of us in the Western world are taught to seek help when symptoms are in full expression and we can't ignore them anymore. Ultimately, our goal is to live in a healthy, balanced way to avoid illness, and when it does arise, we apply the tools and techniques that pull us back to balance within the first few stages. The challenge today is our level of distraction and disconnection from our body/mind communication. To notice that we've strayed away from the stream of well-being requires us to have some skillfulness in body awareness and mindfulness. Imagine how our health would differ if we took heed of the first few signs of an ailment instead of waiting until we have a disaster on our hands?

Qing Li, a Chinese medical doctor in Halifax, says "I wish my patients would come to me ten years earlier so I can help them return to balance with small adjustments. Unfortunately, most finally decide to come to me when their bodies are broken down from stress and disease has consumed their tissues." Our work then, is to address the issue before it takes root and expresses itself as a serious health issue.

Seeds of imbalance and impaired health can manifest themselves not only physically, but mentally as well. If not tended to, a low mood can spiral downward into a deep depression.

For example, Pam had endured a few really tough years, trying to maintain her position at a top university while struggling through a crippling illness. Over time, her attitude toward life went continuously downhill, until one day, her friends confronted her about her "downer perspective and constant complaining." During a yoga class, she became present to the fear of failure that she had masked as brazen negativity in an attempt to stay strong and controlled. With her new awareness, she was able to address her underlying fears and seek proper help for the repair of both her body and her mind, before it grew to the point of clinical depression.

We are habit making machines and our behavior can create positive or negative momentum. Our job is to create as much positive momentum as we can.

The practices taught in this program, serve as sticks in the spokes of the habit wheel. They can stall the momentum long enough to allow us to change directions. Sometimes a negative habit can gain momentum without our awareness of it, until one day, we wake up and realize we're captivated by its power.

Living within the stream of well-being requires us to a) accept who we are and b) honor our limits, which means doing just enough in our work, play, sleep and exercise. Anything done insufficiently or excessively causes imbalance and imbalance is the first phase of any illness. Even a healthy habit can turn toxic if done too much or too little. For example, sleep is essential to our wellbeing, but if done excessively it can depress our system and create lethargy.

Learning about your own unique 'edge' is a concept that will be emphasized in your movement practices throughout this program. Listening to your limits and honoring your edge is part of this journey that you hopefully will continue throughout your life.

How do you know if you're self accepting, honoring your edge and living within the stream of well-being? You feel healthy, happy, and vibrantly alive with strong immunity, balanced emotions and mental clarity.

Here are some other ways that we tend to deny our personal needs, causing us to slide out of the stream of wellbeing. Are any of these familiar to you?

- Agreeing with others when you inwardly disagree
- Masking your true feelings
- Following the crowd when you really don't want to
- Denying yourself of the things you really want to do
- Pushing yourself too hard
- Meeting others needs while ignoring your own
- Not allowing yourself rest or downtime when you need it
- Skipping meals and eating poorly
- Not giving yourself enough sleep

- Spending too much time alone, away from those who love you
- Not exercising or exercising excessively
- Using substances or other indulgences to escape your feelings

THE AYURVEDIC APPROACH TO HEALTH AND HARMONY

Do you notice that sometimes you feel imbalanced but you can't quite trace the reason for it?

We've likely all had times in our lives when we felt a little out of balance and can't quite put our finger on why. By learning what your natural body/mind type is, you can design your life to care for any weaknesses or vulnerabilities within your system. You are currently in the midst of your first major life transition, as you shed your childhood skin and evolve into womanhood. A shift such as this typically comes with hormonal upheaval, causing emotional outbursts, physical symptoms like skin outbreaks and mental confusion.

By identifying your body/mind type, you can learn more about what balance and optimal health feels like for your unique nature and you'll be better able to create a lifestyle that nurtures you best.

Identifying our unique nature is the beginning of self-awareness.

WHAT IS AYURVEDA?

Ayurveda is an Indian science and a unique framework known to be the oldest of any medical system in the world, with a history of Ayurvedic hospitals and colleges going back well over 3,000 years. It addresses illnesses of the body as well as imbalances of the mind.

Ayurveda is not just a system of medicine, but a science of health promotion designed to optimize our well-being and happiness in all aspects of our lives: physically, mentally, emotionally and spiritually.

Through understanding the five elements and how they effect our lives, we can better choose lifestyle habits such as food, exercise, sleep/rest, work and relationships that nourish and balance our entire being.

Ayurveda identifies people's body/mind type by taking into account their physical features and personality traits. It can be exciting and affirming to realize that how we tick and how we relate to the world is explainable under this psychophysical model.

Earth, water, fire, air and space are the five elements considered to be the building blocks of the entire universe, including us humans.

From the combination of these elements, our unique *dosha* or body/mind constitutions arise.

There are 3 *doshas*, or body/mind types. They are similar to the Western framework that categorizes the various body types as ectomorph (equivalent to *vata*), mesomorph (equivalent to *pitta*) and endomorph (equivalent to *kapha*).

THE 3 *DOSHAS*

Vata/Air: the essence of movement, combination of wind and space
Pitta/Fire: the essence of transformation, combination of fire and water

Kapha/Earth: the essence of structure, combination of water and earth

Vata/Air

Qualities	cold, light, dry, irregular, rough, changing, and quick
Body frame	thin, slender frame, light muscles
Weight	low, difficult to gain
Skin	dry, cool and rough
Hair	dry, thin and brittle
Eyes	small and move quickly
Joints	prominent joints, crack easily
Speech	talkative, speak rapidly
Sleep	restless, difficulty getting to sleep
Appetite	irregular
Elimination	slow, frequent constipation and gas
Temperament	active, easily flustered, social
Emotions	enthusiastic, creative, nervous, indecisive
Disturbed by	cold, dry environments, schedule irregularity, excessive physical output, stress of any kind

Symptoms of imbalanced *vata*

- Physical: low body temperature, constipation, fatigue, insomnia, flatulence.
- Mental/emotional: feelings of fear, anxiety, insecurity, impulsiveness, confusion and distracted thought, compulsive activity, incessant talking

Balancing *vata*

Long-term treatment to balance air imbalance could include a consistent, daily manageable schedule, a regulated sleep pattern, increased digestive fire (ginger tea), self massage, gentle yoga, meditation, stress management and peaceful relationships.

In the Western world, we tend to be obsessed with *vata*'s thin, small-framed body type. In reality, *vata* is the most unstable *dosha*, prone to illness and emotional upheaval. Being *vata*, especially the imbalanced *vata* images that we see in the media, is not all it's cracked up to be. For *vatas*, it is essential to stay warm, avoid stress and keep a balanced weight.

Lifestyle changes that nurture Vata/Air

Vata is the type that most readily slides out of balance for all of us, which is why we have a vata imbalanced society (busy, rushing, stressed, reactive, talking vs listening).

- Establish a daily schedule that you can follow with ease
- Eat regular snacks and meals
- Consume warm liquids
- Minimize caffeine and alcohol
- Gentle fluid exercise, like Yoga, Tai Chi, or walking in nature.

- Create a calming evening routine that promotes healthy sleep, which will help to ease the stress response. Take a warm bath by candlelight, read an inspiring book, chat with a friend, cuddle with a pet, do restorative yoga, or drink warm milk with nutmeg or cardamom for digestive support.
- Nurture your senses: play soothing music and burn calming aromatherapy oil
- Take deep, smooth breaths with extended exhalations
- Receive regular body work, like massage or osteopathy

Pitta/Fire

Qualities	hot, light, intense, sharp, acidic and moist
Body frame	medium build, strong muscles
Weight	can quickly gain or lose
Skin	soft, oily and warm
Hair	early greying or balding, oily, blonde or red
Eyes	sharp and bright with a pointed gaze
Joints	medium, moist, loose and flexible
Speech	precise, clear, sometimes forceful
Sleep	moderate, require less than other types
Appetite	strong, can eat high quantities
Elimination	regular, tendency toward loose stools
Temperament	efficient, perfectionistic, intense, leaders
Emotions	passionate, determined, irritable
Disturbed by	high spice, salty and sour foods, excessive heat/sun exposure, sleep disturbances, working too hard

Symptoms of imbalanced *pitta*

- Physical: intense hunger and thirst, indigestion or acid indigestion, skin irritations, rashes or outbreaks, infections
- Mental/emotional: perfectionistic and controlling, feeling angry, agitated or impatient, jealous, critical, competitive, type-A tendency to overwork

Balancing *pitta*

Include foods that are sweet, bitter and astringent (milk, rice, fruit, wheat), minimize spice and caffeine, cooling core temperature, abhyanga, rest, laughter, yoga and meditation. Take steps to relieve stress, and nourish your senses with yummy fragrances, experience natural beauty with hikes, outdoor activities, engage in hobbies and exercises that are non-competitive.

The *pitta* body type, stemming from the fire element, is the only dosha that is hot so it is important that Vata and Kapha assume practices for boosting pitta in their systems. Pitta's, pace yourself so you don't burn out your flame in efforts to change the world!

Kapha/Earth

Qualities	cold, heavy, soft, stable, dull, slow and steady
Body Frame	robust, stocky, solid
Weight	heavy, well-developed bones and muscles
Skin	smooth, pale, white
Hair	thick, dark, lustrous
Eyes	large, calm and kind
Joints	solid, lubricated, can congest
Speech	slow, quiet, deep voice
Sleep	deep and long
Appetite	slow, consistent, can eat less than others
Elimination	sluggish
Temperament	sweet, serene, easy going and supportive
Emotions	affectionate, calm, attached
Disturbed by	cold, oily and heavy foods (dairy, wheat, sweets), damp and cold environments, sedentary lifestyle

Symptoms of imbalanced *kapha*

- Physical: diminished appetite, craving fatty foods, slow digestion, emotional eating and weight gain, congestion, swollen joints, excessive sleep, fatigue and dullness
- Mental/emotional: greed, attachment to others, clinging to the past, feeling dull and depressed, procrastination and a feeling of being stuck, withdrawing from life

Balancing *kapha*

Consume less food, eat foods that are light, dry and hot (minimize carbs), detoxify digestive tract, increase digestive flame with ginger, increase metabolism with rigorous exercise and stimulate your life with spontaneity and exciting entertainment, laugh out loud, take the time for self massage, rise before dawn, get out and socialize.

Here's the thing - Kaphas, trying to be Vata when you're not is like trying to be Asian when you're Caucasian. Kaphas need to know that they are the most stable of all the doshas, so Pittas and Vatas need you to be YOU! Celebrate your curves baby!

From Vata envy to Kapha embodiment; we've disempowered the feminine by making women unnaturally skinny. When women become too thin, the body enters a state of starvation where menstruation ceases to focus on more vital survival functions, creativity and mental clarity decreases, and our overall passion and zest for life diminishes. Our fat phobic culture has done a great disservice to women, since sufficient fat is exactly what we need to thrive in the world, to produce healthy offspring and to effectively feed them. Removing fat from women's constitution is like taking the roar out of a tiger. Imagine a zebra without stripes or a giraffe with no neck? Wouldn't that look silly?

Dysmorphophobia

Dysmorphophobia is the medical term for obsessive body image issues and the fear of a misshapen body. It is very probable that this condition has arisen from our cultural practice of objectifying women's bodies, viewing them as objects to be judged instead of the sacred vehicles for experiencing life that they are. Identifying our dosha, the body type we were born with, can help us to accept our natural shape so that we can devote our energy toward productive endeavors.

If you related most to the *vata* list of qualities, you are more than likely very enthusiastic, jovial, active, creative and constantly changing. When you become stressed however, which you may experience often, you can quickly experience anxiety, nervous tension, fear and reactivity.

If you related most to the *pitta* list of qualities, you are more than likely very passionate, motivated, achievement focused and confident. When you become stressed however, you can be angry, critical, blaming and irritable.

If you related most to the *kapha* list of qualities, you are like cool, calm, reliable and nurturing. When you become stressed, which doesn't happen a lot for you, you may experience depression, dullness, and sluggishness.

When your body/mind type is stable and balanced, you experience health and vitality. When you are out of balance, you may experience any one of the imbalances mentioned above. Wow – this means that cultivating balance requires different measures for each body type. We'll be addressing body imbalances through our movement practices and exploring a few common mental imbalances through our discussions and workshops.

Our changing brains

One thing we know about imbalances or habits of any kind, is that the longer they linger, the harder they are to heal. That is why self-awareness is so important. If your life is a book, you're currently writing the first few chapters. Now is a perfect time for you to be reflecting on your lifestyle habits and where they fit into the stream of well-being. Consider this: the daily practices and habits you lay down now, may very well set the tone for the rest of your life because people don't like change and the mind and body are drawn to sameness and routine. In fact, most adults are employing the same habit patterns and beliefs they've had about themselves since a young age, because they don't realize this most amazing fact: our brains are moldable, like warm clay on a potters wheel! Let's also note that, according to brain researcher Daniel Siegal, the human brain is not fully developed until the mid-twenties, so treating your growing brain with care makes a whole lot of sense.

Through amazing, cutting-edge brain research, we now know that our brains do not remain the same throughout our lives. Our brains actually change, according to:
- How we nourish them (with food, rest, entertainment, music, practices such as meditation and intellectual stimulation)
- The life experiences we have

When we undergo an experience, our brain cells—called neurons—become active, or 'fire'. The brain has one hundred billion neurons. When neurons fire together, they grow new connections between them. Over time, the connections that result from firing, lead to rewiring in the brain. This is incredibly exciting news. It means that we aren't held captive for the rest of our lives by the way our brain works at this moment—we can actually rewire it so that we can be healthier and happier.[8]

A Message from Jenny

When I was born, my earthly form took shape with the predominance of fire, expressed as the Pitta dosha, and air, expressed as the Vata dosha.

This combination has proven to be a tricky dance of opposites, because the fire in me is strong, aggressive and pushes through challenge. However, the Vata, or air side of me, is tender, sensitive and cautious. In a sense, I live within a system that has two opposing needs, which has been the impetus behind my need to seek better balance. After all, we know what happens when fire is let loose in dry windy environments—whoosh, it all goes up in flames!

After years of allowing my fire to consume my more subtle elements, I've learned to temper my fiery, driven nature so it doesn't burn me out entirely. I have also realized how essential it is for me to incorporate more kapha qualities, which I enjoy through meditation, warm foods, rest and nurturing relationships. Enlightened by these understandings, I have learned to manage my inner flame and protect the creative potential of my sensitive Vata constitution.

At first, these concepts may seem a little overwhelming but your relationship with your body is a life long journey, and you can't live without your body. There are NO replacements or trade ins for a broken down body, simply put: no body, no life. Without your health, you really don't have anything.

Just for fun, let's imagine that you started to ignore your best friend or treat her poorly, making fun of her and criticizing her. What do you think would happen to your relationship? It would likely dissolve pretty quickly and the two of you would go your separate ways in no short order. Well ironically, many of us treat our bodies similarly. We ignore our body's need for nutritious food, exercise, oxygen and rest, assuming it will stick around and remain healthy anyway.

We treat our bodies poorly by feeding them processed, fried, or overly rich food, some of us starving them of food or movement. Sometimes we beat them up with harsh exercise regimes. Other times we just completely dissociate from them, trying to convince ourselves that we don't need our bodies at all. That we can live in our heads, consumed by social media, technology and school. Others are used and abused.

How and who you are in your body is one of the most sacred relationships you will ever have, and it is time to start paying attention to the way in which you treat it.

Here's to life balance and to the longest relationship you will ever have,

Jenny

---

[8] Daniel J Seigel MD and Tina Payne Bryson PhD, *The Whole Brain Child* (Bantam Books Trade Paperbacks 2012), 7.

Three Phases of Life

Childhood

According to Ayurvedic medicine, the first phase of life is childhood, from birth to the end of physical development (up to about 16 to 18 years old). Have you ever wondered why babies tend to be chubby and sleep and eat all the time? This phase is governed by the earth element and the *kapha dosha*, as you build physical structure for years to come. It is important in this beginning phase of life to establish healthy lifestyle habits that help to build a reservoir of health and energy for the remainder of one's life. We do this by focusing on the pillars of *swasthi*/health, which are:
1) Good nutrition
2) Nurturing relationships
3) Ample sleep
4) Appropriate exercise

Adolescence is the transition from childhood into adulthood, when we evolve from being a girl to a woman, which is typically marked by the beginning of menstruation.

This is a time when a young woman becomes alive with feminine energy, or the power of creation, Shakti. Just like electricity, which can both light up your home and, if used improperly, can electrocute you, this energy must be properly harnessed in order to be used effectively and not to your detriment. With the awareness of this first major life transition, we can make this time a productive period, instead of one of great strife and upheaval.

We have a wonderful opportunity here to examine our beliefs about being a woman. What does becoming a woman mean to you? Are you afraid of being violated or do you believe in your own strength and in the goodness of the universe? Do you believe we are born innocent and remain that way, despite the cards we've been dealt as children and the mistakes we'll inevitably make along our path?

A school principal taking the Yoga in Schools training program once said, in a conversation about youth, "Instead of looking for poor student behavior and assigning appropriate punishment, I encourage my teachers to catch them doing something good, and applaud their good choices." Instead of focusing on our weaknesses and our mistakes, we could start catching ourselves doing something great and identify ourselves with the positive, rather than the negative.

Are there areas in your life where you could foster more tenderness and positivity toward yourself during your first life transition?

If we are to access our true core power, our flame of creativity and our potential for love, we must begin the process of weeding out the negative beliefs that tell us that as women we are weak, or bad or an object to be used. What beliefs do you hold about what it means to be a woman in the world?

This female energy that is now flowing through you is nothing short of the powerful energy of creation itself, which is why we need to learn to deal with it skillfully.

What are some ways in which girls express their feminine energy in an unhealthy or unskilled way?

What are some ways in which we could harness this powerful feminine force to propel us in a positive, self-respecting and nurturing direction?

Reflect on your own transition from childhood to adulthood. What emotions are surfacing for you? How are you acknowledging this transition? What do you need during this time that you are not receiving, if anything? How can you give that to yourself now?

Womanhood

The second phase is the age of *pitta*, governed by the fire element. This is the time when we transform from living just for ourselves to becoming a provider of life and change agent, be it as a mother or a business person or another life-supporting role. The Girl on Fire program is designed to prepare you for the second phase of your life, which begins around age 18 until about the age of 50.

If a young girl has had a secure upbringing that fostered self-esteem and healthy lifestyle habits, she will enter the world with the perception that it is a kind, benign place to be. Sometimes, somehow we assume the opposite belief that the world is dangerous and malicious. If we are to live our second and third phases of life with a sense of freedom, possibility and joy, we must heal that perception so we can attract goodness into our lives. Now is a great time to learn to trust that the forces of the universe are conspiring on your behalf and supporting you in reaching your fullness.

Can you imagine what this upcoming phase of womanhood will be like?

What are your fears?

What excites you about this phase?

What are your dreams for this phase?

The Wise Woman

The third phase of life is called the wisdom years, governed by wind and the *vata dosha*. All other relationships are mirrors of our relationship with ourselves, and if we have cultivated self-love and understanding, we'll have rich and lasting connections into old age. At this phase we transform into being a mother to all, a source of love and guidance beyond our own self-consciousness and a force for justice and goodness.

According to the yoga tradition, every creature that is born lives with the reality that she/he will one day die. This is the phase of life where we prepare to move on to next realm of existence, trading in the body we've been granted for a whole new unknown adventure. If we have treated it respectfully and lived a life of balance, our body is likely to serve us well into old age.

Reflect on a grandparent or an older mentor who has demonstrated beauty and wisdom in their elder years. How do you want to feel in the final phase of your life?

CHANGE VS. TRANSFORMATION

It's important to know the difference between change and transformation as we transition through our various stages. Change is something you can do temporarily, like changing into your jeans in the morning, and then changing back into sweats in the evening. Transformation however, is a permanent inner shift. Once you peel a banana and toss it into the blender, there is no way of piecing the banana back together into its original form. You are not the same once you go through your transformational periods. Your awareness will be altered permanently. And hopefully, if it's done respectfully, altered positively toward the betterment of yourself and the world.

Ideally, a Girl on Fire uses her youthful, fiery energy to transform into the best version of herself, and not an attempted version of something or someone else. Your job through this first transition is to gain a deeper understanding of who you are, and your unique abilities, strengths and gifts. In fact, your highest responsibility in life is to express your unique self and share your gifts with the world in a way that is kind to you and all other beings.

> Your job is not to do someone else's soul purpose, even if you can do it perfectly, but to fulfill your own dreams and heart's desire, even if you do it imperfectly. ~ Bhagavad Gita

OMWORK

This week, watch our Girl on Fire Pre-Teen video on Chemical influences and hormone health.

As was mentioned above, it is important in the beginning phase of life to establish healthy lifestyle habits that help to build a reservoir of health and energy for the remainder of your life. For your omwork, you are invited to focus on one of the following health themes and journal about your insights:
- Good nutrition
- Nurturing relationships
- Ample sleep
- Exercise —for example, a 20 minute brisk walk in nature.

Remember, we can only make positive changes in our lives if we are aware of the way in which we're living now. Self-awareness might possibly be the most important virtue you ever cultivate in your life, and one you can spend your whole life developing.

SELF-ACCEPTANCE AND INNER-BEAUTY EXERCISE

Go home and spend 10 minutes in the mirror, gazing into your eyes, noticing the scope of your inner dialogue: the criticism, the self-hatred, the glimpses of joy, the sparkle in your eye. **Metacognition** is the practice of observing one's inner dialogue and then transforming it. Keep gazing until you can count out 10 things you love about yourself, we are so used to being stingy with ourselves, now is the time to practice being generous, kind and truly acknowledging of the divine beauty you've been granted.

SELF-LOVE QUIZ

This quiz is designed to encourage you to become more mindful of how you engage with yourself on a daily basis. The more awareness we can bring to the way in which we treat ourselves, the more capable we are of making positive changes that foster self worth and self love, resulting in greater health and happiness.
Studies show that people who are more compassionate and loving to themselves, experience more life success, more resilience, greater relationship fulfillment and deeper levels of inner peace. Mark your answers on a scale of 1 to 5.

1	2	3	4	5
Always	Mostly	Sometimes	Rarely	Never

Questions:

1) Are you gentle with yourself throughout the day? ____
2) Does your inner dialogue nurture your wellbeing? ____
3) Do you ever do little acts of kindness for yourself? ____
4) Do you let yourself receive a complement? ____
5) Do you believe that being loving and gentle with yourself is healthy and natural? ____
6) Do you respectfully listen to your own needs (instead of ignoring them and putting others needs before yours)? ____

Add up your score. The answers to these questions may reveal your level of self-love and the degree to which you care for yourself.

If you scored anywhere between 21 and 30, you may be living in sparse, barren love conditions that require a big self-care renovation. Not to worry, you were born with love for yourself and therefore you still hold the memory of it inside. Life has just taken you off course a bit. Through this work, you will unlearn the lies you were told about yourself and discover the truth of who you really are, which is totally and immensely lovable.

If your score was between 12 and 20, you may be sometimes good to yourself, and sometimes rotten, so there are still improvements required in your degree of generosity with yourself.

If your score was less than 11, congratulations, you are living with a healthy amount of self-love, which tends to translate into good health physically, mentally, emotionally and spiritually.

LIFELONG GUIDE TO EATING AND LIVING

When you're hungry, eat until you're comfortably full.
When you're thirsty, drink until you're sated.
When you're tired, nap until you wake up.
When you're antsy, move your body.
When you're stressed, release it.

Imagine what your life would look like if you heeded the messages buried within the intelligence of your body.

Minimize Flunc Foods[9]

- Frozen
- Leftovers
- Unnatural
- Nuked
- Canned

Maximize whole foods

Get them fresh from their source, local and unprocessed. If it doesn't resemble its original form, go to its source. Fresh fruit has more nutrients, hydration and energy than packaged fruit gummies, which likely have added sugar, colouring, etc.

Affirmation

When my body and mind are stable and balanced, I experience health and vitality.

I respect my body and care for it as a most precious gift.

I recognize that my body constitution is different from anyone else's and I celebrate my uniqueness.
I admit that it requires dedication to take care of my body, and I am worthy of this time and attention.

Personal additions:

Physical Posture

Downward Dog

---

[9] Deepak Chopra MD, Perfect Health Program, (Chopra Centre)

Mindful Movement Class - Week 2

NOTE: This is the Mindful Movement Class to accompany Week 2. For consistency and ease, we recommend the video series of these classes available at www.GirlOnFire.ca.

Weekly theme – Self Awareness
Child's Pose Rabbit Pose Plankasana with two part breathing Cobra Pose to Child's Pose vinyasa **Feature Posture:** Downward Dog Downward Dog to Upward Dog vinyasa Downward Dog with leg lifts Crescent Lunge Warrior 1 to Bowing Warrior Plankasana (or Table) to Side Plank on hand and foot Wild Thing Downward Dog to Mountain Pose Holding up the Earth flow Earth and Sky flow Shoulder Shrugs and rotations Shake it out **Partner Posture:** sitting back to back, interlock arms and press up to standing and back down to sitting a number of times. Seated Pigeon/Rock the baby Seated Forward Bend to Draw the Bow Savasana/Relaxation Pose
Girl on Fire closing To acknowledge the three centers of Power, Love and Insight: Rise to sitting and bring palms together. Lift hands so that thumbs touch the mid eye point and say: "Guided by insight" Now draw hands to heart, one palm on heart center in the middle of the chest and the other palm resting on top of the first hand and say: "I listen to my heart's desire" Now take the top hand and slide it down so it rests on the navel, with the first hand remaining on the heart and say: "And take positive, powerful action in the world"

Notes

Week 3 – Self-Worth

This week's focus is to gain a deeper understanding of:
- The ego
- Definition of self-worth and self-esteem
- Introduction to the *chakra* system and the fire centre, *manipura*
- Lifestyle habits that influence our inner flame, *sattvic* living
- How shame can snuff your flame

THE EGO

The Ego is a term that psychology has been analyzing and yogis have been transcending for millennia. Many of us journey through life, completely identifying with the ego, not realizing there is anything beyond it. But the ego, or more specifically, the neurotic ego, is actually the veil that can cover the joy of life.

In the yoga tradition, the ego is known as Ahamkara, or "I am-ness." It is the constructed concept of ourselves that defines us as separate from others, and relies on information from the outside world to affirm its identity. The ego survives on the premise that we must build our outer image to be worthy and respected. Therefore, it is driven by performance, perfection and possessions.

While some schools of yoga claim that the ego is ignorant and must be transcended, it's valuable to view the ego as having two aspects. After all, we can't live without it. The part of our psyche that ensures we have all our clothes on in the morning before we leave the house is the same part that wants to protect us and keep us safe from harm. We'll call this our healthy ego. The risk with the ego is that, if given free reign within the mind, it can sometimes go a bit overboard.

The neurotic ego, known as our false self, is fed by what others say about us and how they perceive us. The neurotic ego is constantly grasping for approval and validation, telling us that if we amass more clothes, cars, shoes, music or whatever the latest gismo is, then we'll feel complete. The neurotic ego is an ever-hungry belly.

The interesting thing about the neurotic ego is that it depends on physical form, which we know is in constant change. Have you ever bought a new shirt that you absolutely loved, and in a few months its color faded and so did its appeal? We cling to our bodies in the same way.

Because the ego is always outsourcing its worth through outside validation, it lacks inner substance and therefore has no stability or foundation. But when we relate to our ego with awareness and compassion, we start to develop our healthy ego by seeing the vast existence beyond brand names, others' opinions and our obsession with the physical world.

What is our true nature? Our true nature is completely free and unlimited, full of joy and vibrancy. Our truest self is infinitely creative and capable of just about anything.

We're living through an interesting ego identified pandemic, where our society is consumed with the belief that if you have more money, status and glossy beautiful friends in high places, you're somehow better than your neighbor. It is understood that after striving our whole lives, when we reach the top of this illusory rank, we will be rewarded with everlasting happiness. Unfortunately, we see just the opposite happening; wealthy, popular, beautiful people living lives of despair and emptiness.

Author Clarissa Pinkola Estés speaks of her wild Aunt Edna, in the "Power of the Crone", who used to tell her "Don't make creation too small." We do that, don't we? We change and contract to fit into some external ideal, believing the media's promise that happiness can only be experienced by fitting the mold. As we begin to wake up and realize the value of our healthy ego, we realize we're not honoring the brilliance of creation, which made us all different and unique for a reason.

Through yoga, your true self will gradually be revealed, and when it is, you will then experience the infinite joy that comes from truly loving yourself. This awakening is a homecoming of sorts, like coming home to a warm pot of stew on the stove, full of nourishment for you to draw from when needed.

Living with an egoic perspective, we build our house on sand by fully identifying with the ever-changing aspects of life, like success and beauty. As the winds begin to blow and challenge arise, we then find our house quickly crumbling beneath the pressure because we lack the solid foundation of self-worth.

When we compare our ego identity with other ego identities, the inevitable outcome is that someone wins and someone has to lose. Soon we have a life that is totally identified with false labels and masks, when in reality they are the illusions of all that we are not. Consumed with the illusion of these falsities, an inner void creeps into our souls. Our ego quite literally 'Edges God Out' and alienates us from any source of true and lasting happiness.

As an impressionable young woman inundated by media messages that use women to sell material goods, it is easy to conclude that beauty and sex appeal are the ways to get attention and get ahead in the world. These images incubate in our psyche and mould our views of what it takes to become a respected, successful woman in the world.

If we're not aware of their influence, we unconsciously compare ourselves to media images, and then in most cases, assume that we're too large or too ugly. With that, we buy into the media messages and believe that if we can only get it right, by starving ourselves here and sculpting our bodies there, our perfect appearance will earn us unconditional love and alleviate all suffering. As Caroline Myss says, we learn that our face and frame become our fortune.

Throughout this program you will be encouraged to reframe this limiting and diminishing perspective of what it means to be a woman today and realize that you are worthy of healthy and respectful relationships just the way you are.

What we know

- Girls desperately need better role models. In a recent study conducted by the Canadian Women's Foundation, over 60% of people say celebrities are the primary role models for girls. In comparison, only 36% said girls look up to their parents the most, and almost no one said girls look up to professionals such as scientists or writers.[10]
- if your role model is a celebrity, you will most likely learn your primary value comes from how you look, rather than your intelligence, kindness, or creativity. To reach their full potential, girls must have female role models who are respected for something other than looking sexy[11].

Self-Worth or Self-Esteem?

The solar plexus at the core of your body hosts your sense of self (self-worth) and self-esteem. It is also where your gut-instinct resides. That's the part of you that recognizes safety and danger without having to think about it. In anatomical terms, this part of the body is called the enteric nervous system. This is one of our unique female gifts, like having your own internal bodyguard. But, according to author Caroline Myss, with low self-esteem and lack of trust in yourself, it's almost impossible to access. Without a sense of self, we become like a boat without a rudder, floating from one passing fad to another in an attempt to find wholeness.

Let's identify the difference between self-worth and self-esteem. Your self-worth can be viewed as your internal sense of who you are and your value, while your self-esteem is related to the way you feel about yourself with regards to the outside world, the way you act, the way you look and the way you are perceived by others.

Our self-worth is the feeling (*bhava*) we have for ourselves in terms of importance, belonging and personal identity. As you can imagine, without a sense of personal value or importance, it's impossible to fully shine as a Girl on Fire because our inner flame is extinguished by our own perception. It's like the difference between a mannequin and a real-life human being. The mannequin can look totally real, especially from a distance, but once we're up close, we realize that it's just a shell. Have you met anyone like that, well put together on the outside but somehow vacant on the inside?

Studies show that seeking external validation actually has mental-health risks. People who rely on outside validation to affirm their self-worth are more likely to experience stress, depression and anxiety. One interesting study shows that students who were most focused on academic performance encountered more conflict and stress, without higher grades. Students who based their self-worth on external sources were also shown to have higher levels of alcohol and drug use, as well as more symptoms of eating disorders.

The good news is that students who relied on inner strengths felt better about themselves, received higher marks and were less likely to use drugs and alcohol or to develop eating disorders. Bottom line? Chasing around outside sources to fill your inner tank of self-worth is hazardous to your physical and mental health and doesn't work, at least not long term.

---

[10] "Facts About Girls in Canada" Canadian Women's Foundation, accessed September 2016, http://canadianwomen.org/facts-about-girls
[11] Ibid

When our self-worth is adequately constructed, the light of our internal flame can be seen through our body language (in our eyes and our actions) and the warmth of our inner flame can be felt through the expressions of our words and our emotions. When we develop our sense of self-worth, we will naturally exude self-esteem because they are intricately connected.

A woman with solid self-worth and self-esteem moves with confidence and ease and lives with passion and purpose.

To be a Girl on Fire, we may need to undergo a paradigm shift, a restructuring of our core belief system. We must stop measuring our sense of self according to the fluctuating standards of the fashion industry, or someone else's opinion. We must turn away from outside measurements that can threaten our sense of intrinsic value and focus our attention on loving who we are, as we are. Our challenge is to focus on who we are, not what we are. You are a who, not a what☺. In other words, you are a person of great value, not an object for display or to be used for other people's pleasure or gain.

One of the main culprits that erode our self-worth is the inner critical voice. Along with the foundation of self awareness, our sense of self-worth is an essential virtue to develop, for without it we'll never experience the true bliss of achieving our life goals and we'll never feel the amazing depths of love that's available to us. This is why, if your self-worth is lacking luster, it is crucial that you take it on as your top priority. After all, YOU'RE WORTH IT!

One of the most important things you can do for yourself is to learn to minimize the fire-snuffing factors in your life and amplify the fire fueling factors that help you to build your house on solid ground.

Chakras and The Fire Essence

To get started on that goal, let's discuss where fire lives in our physical bodies. Our bodies are made up of physical organs, tissues and cells that have qualities of the five elements of nature: earth, water, fire, air and space. Our bodies, however, are more than just solid form.

They are also comprised of thousands of channels of energy that flow throughout the body and around it. There are seven main areas where these channels converge, which ancient masters called *chakras*, or concentrated energetic centres. When a person is healthy and balanced, these centers spin freely. The qualities we are cultivating within this Girl on Fire program, have a specific residence within the body's energetic structure. Let's take a closer look at where they lie and where, specifically, self-confidence is nurtured within the yogic energetic framework.

The most commonly known chakras

Our first *chakra*, related to the *kapha dosha*, is the root gate, which means our point of connection to Mother Earth and our tribe or family. It is also where we connect to our history on an ancestral level. It is at this centre where we access power from our root connections to the past and the earth.

Our second *chakra* is where our centre of gravity resides. Many traditions have identified this region of the body as a significant center of power, for example in martial arts this is called the *hara* and in Chinese healing, it is referred to as the dantien or reservoir of vital energy. This region relates to our physical vitality, sensuality and sexual energy, which has the creative power to produce new life. Like the watery nature of the womb, it is characterized by the water element, which is adaptable and fluid. This center of the sacral plexus enables us to endure challenge without being thrown off base.

Our solar plexus, related to the *pitta dosha* of fire, is often referred to as our place of the shining gem. It is our action centre, where we exert our will and personal power to act in the world. Our self-esteem and confidence are experienced here. Proper action occurs when we blend passion from our heart centre with the stability of our lower *chakras*.

Our heart centre, related to the *vata dosha* of air, is the juncture between the lower centres and the upper centres, where our true essence (the purity of our being) resides. Our deepest dreams live here as well as the vast language of emotions. At our healthiest, we exude love and harmony from this centre.

Our throat centre, related to the element of space, is where we harness our energy for self expression, speaking out into the world our desires and our innate gifts. It is here where we also express our needs, which requires an established self-esteem to do so effectively and confidently.

Our third-eye centre, which exists beyond the physical elements, is where we connect to the infinite power of the universe through our sixth sense of intuition. When this region is open, we see beyond the physical world, tapping into our clear-seeing, sensing abilities and tap into our inner GPS.

The seventh *chakra* resides at the crown of the head and is the point at which we experience oneness with the creative force of the Universe. At this centre, all separation ceases and we become immersed in the blissful reality that we are all one. We move from an 'us versus them' mentality to just US.

When our centres are balanced and harmonious, we can impact the world and influence change through our power, love and insight.

LOCATION	ASANA	COLOR	SOUND	ELEMENT	PSYCHOLOGICAL FUNCTION
7) SAHASRARA (cosmic Consciousness)					
Crown of Head	Meditation	Diamond White	OM	VOID (Beyond Elements)	Integration of whole being, Sense of wholeness, Peace, Faith, Sense of purpose for existence. Transcendence of mundane reality, Oneness, "I KNOW—I AM"
6) AJNA (conscious Awareness)					
Space Between Eyebrows	Cobra	Indigo	AUM	MIND	Insight, Capacity to visualize & understand reality, Creative ideas, Capacity to implement visions and ideas. "I SEE"
5) VISHUDDUHA (Surrender)					
Throat	Neck stretches	Blue	HAM	SPACE	Capacity to take in nourishment, Ability to ask for & receive one's needs. Taking responsibility, Ability to speak truthfully who you are. "I SPEAK"

LOCATION	ASANA	COLOR	SOUND	ELEMENT	PSYCHOLOGICAL FUNCTION
4) ANAHATA (unconditional love)					
Heart	Yoga Mudra	Green	YAM	AIR	Capacity to love all life, to see inner beauty in all without expecting anything in return. Trust. No longer cut off from self or others. "I LOVE"
3) MANIPURA (connectedness)					
Solar Plexus	Boat	Yellow	RAM	FIRE	Feeling of belonging; Capacity to have a fulfilling emotional life, Connectedness to Mother, Will, Power. "I CAN"
2) SWADISTHAN (creation)					
Lower Abdomen (Sacrum)	Pelvic Tilt	Orange	VAM	WATER	Quality and Quantity of Sexual Energy, Creativity, Vitality, Sensuality. "I FEEL"
1) MULADHARA (security)					
Coccyx/Anus	Head to Knee	Red	LAM	EARTH	Quantity of physical energy, Will to live in physical reality, Grounding, Survival. Capacity to experience

LOCATION	ASANA	COLOR	SOUND	ELEMENT	PSYCHOLOGICAL FUNCTION
					physical pleasure/sensation "I AM HERE"

In particular, let's take a closer peek at the manipura, our fire centre.

LOCATION	ASANA	COLOR	SOUND	ELEMENT	PSYCHOLOGICAL FUNCTION
3) MANIPURA (connectedness)					
Solar Plexus	Boat	Yellow	RAM	FIRE	Feeling of belonging; Capacity to have a fulfilling emotional life, Connectedness to Mother, Will, Power. "I CAN"

It is at this centre where we access our self-worth, inner strength and will, and it takes the boldness of the fire element to exert ourselves in the world.

This centre is supported when we feel connected to others through a sense of belonging.

This centre is also connected to the third eye, in that our third centre sense is sight, connecting us to our intuition, our gut knowing, which is one of our greatest female gifts (men do have intuition but they have to work for it, whereas ours is wired into our being).

The *manipura* is the area in the body where we digest not only food, but life experiences, transforming it all into fuel for our lives. This digestive process requires fire in the belly, known *in Ayurvedic medicine* as *agni*, in order to turn our food into proper fuel. If our *agni* is low, caused by inactivity, poor breathing, poor nutrition or dehydration, we'll have trouble digesting and we may produce toxins instead of the desired nourishment. We use this inner flame not only for food digestion but also for digesting emotional content, ideally absorbing the good and consciously releasing the negative.

This process of transformation, whereby a substance is transformed into another essence, is reflected in the three key phases of a woman's life. Each phase is related to a *chakra* and a *dosha*, with the childhood years related to the *kapha dosha*. As a Girl on Fire, you are virtually transitioning into your *pitta* season of life, between the ages of 20-50, so this is your time to use your past as a springboard, harness your intuition, listen to your heart's desire and take action that is aligned with your deepest dreams. In other words, this is truly your time to shine like a diamond!

Fire Snuffing-factor—Shame

Shame is the intensely painful feeling or experience of believing we are flawed and therefore unworthy of acceptance and belonging. ~ Brené Brown

A Message from Jenny

When I was about eight years old, we dropped by a department store on our way home from Dad's school. As the acting Vice Principal, he had had a demanding day and his patience was worn thin. As I browsed the shelves for colorful items that awakened my wanting instinct, a beautiful pair of fuchsia gloves jumped out at me and I just had to have them. After pulling out all the stops—the eyelash flash, the logical explanation and finally, the hard lined negotiations of offering my allowance for the next month—my father refused. When he said, "No, they're too expensive" I was devastated and spent a few moments hanging my head in defeat. But the more I thought about it, the angrier I felt, and you can't keep a determined girl down.

Back at the shelf, as I reluctantly returned the beautiful fuchsia gloves to their home beside the rows of winter accessories, I noticed another pair. They were similar but much more boring but a few bucks cheaper. So without hesitation, I decisively acted on my stroke of brilliance and peeled off the price tag from the boring gloves and meticulously placed it over the more expensive gloves of preference. Dad was too tired and pre-occupied with his own shopping to notice that the gloves I brought back were the same, believing my story that I'd found another cheaper pair that perhaps we could afford.

My plan would have gone off without a hitch had it not been for my older siblings, who must have been observing the dramatic events unfold. They told Dad what I had done the moment we closed the door on our old red sedan. His typical calm, relaxed demeanor suddenly shifted as his youngest child rattled his ancestral family standard of integrity. My little body instantly started to sizzle with adrenalin and my belly began to tighten with fear, realizing I was in for some kind of severe punishment. He grabbed me by the arm of my coat instead of my hand, which was a clear gesture of distain and purposeful distance.

As he dragged me back into the department store, he muttered under his breath, "I deal with this kind of behavior all day and then I get this with you? No child of mine commits crime. You're going to learn your lesson here and now!"

Still in the dark about what my punishment was, I kept up as best I could as he stomped up the stairs to the manager's office, my little feet barely touching the floor. After a few intent knocks on the door, a dignified man greeted us and invited us into his office. Standing there in a rage, Dad demanded that I tell the man what I had done and apologize immediately. Terrified and ashamed, I did my best to speak but the words were muffled by the uncontainable sobs exploding out of my mouth. While I could tell the manager understood my father's intentions, his overwhelming response to the painful situation was one of compassion and tenderness toward me.

As an administrator at a rough inner city school, I can see now that his strong reaction to my clever attempt to claim the gloves of my dreams was an effort to stamp out any inclination I might have of ever stepping outside the lines of the law. I bet his deepest fear in that moment was the prospect of having to deal with the same issues at home as he was dealing with at school. But my young mind was not capable of rationalizing the situation and seeing his point of view.

Had he stopped and asked for clarification first and then taken the time to explain what theft was and why my actions were inappropriate, I might have fallen asleep that night with the understanding that my behavior was unmistakably unlawful, but that I was still a totally lovable child. Unfortunately, that experience left me with a deep feeling of shame, like a big chunk was chipped off of my inner jewel of self-worth. I fell asleep that night believing that Dad was right, that I was indeed a bad girl who couldn't be trusted, and part of me was afraid of what I might do next. I began to distrust my judgment and myself. Worst of all, I fell asleep hating who I was and wanting to get away from me, but there was no where else to live.

I'm sure you can relate to my early experience of shame. Can you recall your own? What was your experience of it? Perhaps your face blushed and you avoided eye contact with others in an attempt to hide your unworthiness. Maybe you wanted to disappear completely, or take a shower to wash off the inescapable feeling of self-distain.

The journey of healing these wounded parts of ourselves requires us to identify the masks and shields we create to conceal our inadequacies. We all need to feel worthy and loved in order to function, and if we don't, we somehow find ways of numbing ourselves to kill the pain before the feeling of unworthiness kills us.

As scary as it was for me, my own healing process involved peeling back the layers of protection I had built around my heart to conceal the shame I felt about being me. Through that process, I realized that I am indeed, just like everyone else, completely worthy of being loved. And with that awakening, came a new capacity to love others wholeheartedly. When we let go of shame, we gain the gift of human connection.

Don't let shame rule your life. You're way too important for that!

Jenny

In the book *Mother-Daughter Wisdom*, Dr. Christiane Northrup says shame is defined as a painful feeling arising from the awareness of something dishonorable or improper.

Growing up, it is very important to experience the emotion of shame, as it helps us become aware of our actions and how they impact others, according to Northrup. Shame teaches us the difference between appropriate and inappropriate behavior, after all. If we didn't have this distinction we'd see 15-year-olds pulling temper tantrums on the floor to get a need met.

As icky as it is, shame is an important part of our emotional development. It is known to be one of the most painful emotions because it implies that we are unworthy of living. As a result, it is a feeling that most of us will do just about anything to avoid, including lying (I was out when this happened) or blame (the dog did it!).

Some of us were shown the difference between appropriate and inappropriate action in a way that preserved our sense of self worth. For example, a parent who respectfully removes her child at a party and whispers a more skillful way of dealing with toy stealing. This child is then able to experience shame without robbing her of her fundamental self-esteem.

Have you ever had an experience of shame that left your self-esteem intact?

Other times, however, we were taught about shame in a way that degraded our sense of who we are, diminishing our self-esteem. For example, after walking out of a store with a pair of earrings she couldn't live without, a parent might berate her daughter in front of a crowd by saying "You thief! You are such a bad girl for stealing these."

Have you ever had an experience of shame that negatively affected your self-esteem?

Can you see the difference in these approaches? The first one allows for the natural occurrence of mistakes, while respectfully guiding appropriate behavior. Here, shame is not enmeshed with self-esteem. The shame is addressed and one's self-esteem remains intact.

The second approach belittles the person by permeating one's self-esteem with shame. Instead of just identifying the inappropriate behavior, the shame is coupled with the feeling of being a bad person, which has negative and lasting effects on the child's entire character.

We now know that using shame as a way of disciplining children creates a separation between their minds and bodies, which can lead to depression and a lack of interest in life.

> Shaming a child in an imbalanced and unhealthy way can damage her sense of joy, independence, self esteem and bodily acceptance. [12]

Instead of simply identifying a behavior as inappropriate in a given situation, we assume the belief that there is something inherently wrong with us. The trouble with this is that many of us carry shame into our adult years, believing that we are unworthy, broken or bad in some way. This breeds low self-esteem and often manifests into addictive or obsessive behavior in order to somehow manage these painful feelings.

Perhaps you know someone who struggles with an addiction of some kind. The cycle of addiction is often fueled by shame. We feel such shame for being 'bad' or 'inadequate' that we desperately turn to our addictive habits to relieve the pain, which only feeds the negative self-destructive cycle. Viewing addiction this way, it's a bit easier to have compassion for those caught in this painful self-fulfilling prophecy, isn't it?

According to shame researcher Brené Brown, "Shame is so powerful that we sometimes feel shame just talking about shame." The less we know about shame, the more power it seems to have, affecting every aspect of our lives "from our appearance, body image, motherhood, family, parenting, money and work, mental and physical health, addiction, sex, aging and religion." That just about covers every part of our lives, doesn't it? As an emotion we all experience, shame can erode our self esteem in devastating ways, leading to what Brown calls the by-products of shame—fear, blame and disconnection.

Becoming more aware of how shame affects us is an important step in managing its harmful affects. Brown refers to shame resilience as the process of recognizing shame and then learning to grow from it instead of being stunted by it. It seems then that our work as human beings is to become more compassionately self-aware of destructive emotions such as shame, and then become more skilled at processing them as they surface.

The following statement is counter to almost every other message you will receive in the world around you:

Your worth as a young woman is not measured by the clothes you wear, the size of your breasts, your academic grades or your popularity. Your worth as a young woman is ultimately not up for debate because you are alive and therefore, have value, period. Since you have been granted life, with a body, a mind and an essence to animate that body, you not only have permission to be here, but also a responsibility to be totally you. Now is the time for you to claim your right to live with self-worth, and when you do, the light of your heart will freely shine out to the world, inspiring others with its radiance.

Take time to reflect on this statement in your journal. Read it carefully and observe your reactions to it. Discuss it with other women.

OMWORK

Spend a day with your journal, and every time you notice your inner critic express herself, jot down the belief or phrase. Also record any random positive thoughts you have throughout the day. At the end of the day, read through what you've written and take inventory on the quality of your inner dialogue. Changing your inner dialogue from the inner critical voice to the inner compassionate voice is essential work for cultivating self-worth and esteem.

---

[12] Christiane Northrup, M.D., *Mother-Daughter Wisdom*, (Bantam trade paperback edition April 2006), 178.

Craft activity: Your self-worth can be viewed as your inner flame, a house built on solid ground with solid beams, a car with a V6 engine or a flower with a beautiful inner essence. What analogy would you use to describe a strong self-worth? This week you are invited to create an image or design an art piece that reflects your self-worth and bring it to class next week.

Abhyanga: Learning to care for ourselves and cherish our bodies is an important way to affirm the intention to foster self-worth and feel good. *Abhyanga*, the practice of self-massage, is a self-nourishing technique that comforts the body, the mind and your deeper essence. If you want respect outside, you must create an environment of respect inside and *abhyanga* performed with a loving attitude can help us get there.

See Appendix A for Abhyanga instructions.

Affirmations

A woman with self-worth moves with confidence and ease and lives with passion and purpose.

I say "no" with certainty if I find myself in a situation that disrespects my comfort levels or balance.

Today, I release the destructive emotion of shame and I start fresh, with self love in my heart.

Moving and stretching my body each day helps me to live vibrantly with energy and enjoyment.

Personal additions:

Physical Posture

Self-selected posture from the chakra chart.

Mindful Movement Class - Week 3

NOTE: This is the Mindful Movement Class to accompany Week 3. For consistency and ease, we recommend the video series of these classes available at www.GirlOnFire.ca.

Weekly theme – Self Worth
Fire breathing Arm vinyasa to awaken breathing. Qi ball to prayer position, set intention. Cross Pose Breath of Joy Sun Salutation, slowly Plankasanas lifting one foot at a time and then on forearms. Horse Stance facing long side of mat The Sun returns to its origin Wide legged forward bend with arm variations Warrior 1, hands start at lower dantien and slide up the stream of wellbeing Warrior 3 **Partner Posture:** Warrior 3 in three's Earth and Sky flow Gather and Ground flow Yogic bicycle Half bridge Apanasana to supine pigeon Savasana/Relaxation Pose with hands in yoni mudra **Feature Posture:** Self-selected posture from the chakra chart
Girl on Fire closing To acknowledge the three centers of Power, Love and Insight: Rise to sitting and bring palms together. Lift hands so that thumbs touch the mid eye point and say: *"Guided by insight"* Now draw hands to heart, one palm on heart center in the middle of the chest and the other palm resting on top of the first hand and say: *"I listen to my heart's desire"* Now take the top hand and slide it down so it rests on the navel, with the first hand remaining on the heart and say: *"And take positive, powerful action in the world"*

Notes

Week 4 – Confidence

This week's focus is to gain deeper understanding of:
- Internal and external living
- Beauty myths
- How to cultivate confidence

STORY OF SWARUPA, AND OUR GIRL ON FIRE POTENTIAL

There's a beautiful tale in Vedic literature that illustrates who we really are. In a forest in India, a lioness gives birth to a little lion cub. Shortly thereafter, the mother unfortunately dies.

After trying to wake up her mother, the cub wanders off and gets lost searching for food. Feeling tired and hopeless, the cub eventually comes upon a sheep feeding her young. She is quickly accepted among the sheep and grows up as one of them. Naturally, she does not know she is really a lion, even though she feels strange at times because she has trouble bleating and grass is hard for her to digest. But she does not know any better.

One day, while the sheep are grazing as usual, a big lion comes roaring after them. The sheep is terrified, along with the lion cub and they all run away bleating. The big lion stops in surprise at seeing a lion cub afraid of him and bleating like a sheep. He grabs the lion cub in his mouth and carries her away into the jungle. The lion explains to the frightened cub that he is not going to eat her because she is a lion, but that it is not acceptable for lions to be in the company of sheep. The cub can not grasp what the lion is telling her and just keeps repeating, "Don't eat me, please!"

The lion knows then that the cub is not aware of who she truly is. The lion takes her to a nearby river and invites her to look at her reflection in the water. The cub at last accepts that the lion is right. Instantly she relaxes, realizing who she really is. She even begins walking confidently like a lion, instead of sauntering like a sheep. She stops bleating and starts to roar like her fellow lionesses.

Most of us live out our whole lives, not realizing our true selves. We are surrounded by people who are unaware of their fullest potential and the infinite opportunities of life, as this tale shows us. And so, we learn to settle for mediocrity, and we join the flock of sheep.

As a Girl on Fire, you are given the chance to step out from the flock and examine your interests to understand what truly lights you up. Once your brilliance is acknowledged, you can live out your own destiny with confidence and self-respect. But in order to follow your heart, you must abandon the need for outward approval. Letting go of the need to please everyone else will allow you to drop into the deep well of truth within. Today, let's begin to live from the inside out, instead of from the outside in, which is so prevalent in our culture today.

A Girl on Fire is a girl with confidence in herself. Without confidence, one's inner flame is barely seen. But when a woman has confidence, she glows with a beauty that shines from the inside out, she turns heads, she commands respect and she lives on her own terms.

Internally Referenced Living

> "Happiness is your nature. It is not wrong to desire it. What is wrong is seeking it outside when it is inside." Ramana Maharshi

People who live their lives with the awareness of their inner self, are living what we call an internally referenced life. They know that their strengths and weaknesses together make up who they are and they live with a deep acceptance of that, while knowing that their strengths and weaknesses will evolve as they grow. This inner contentment shines through them as love and light and people are naturally drawn to them. When we accept ourselves and love who we are, we become very attractive to others.

Our work is to find out who we are, and then choose to love ourselves, as we are, as we grow. As teens, we want so badly to fit in that we often become anyone our peers want us to be: pretty, loud, rude, arrogant, even a bully. Through contemplation and quiet time, you can begin to reconnect with your true essence. Once we've recaptured our true essence, we've uncovered our greatest source of power.

Sometimes on the path, we may find ourselves intimidated by others' opinions and limiting beliefs about us. Our challenge and opportunity (those two words mean the same as each other in Chinese, by the way) is to turn up the volume of our inner voice so that we can follow our own inner compass and not the fears or judgments of others.

A Message from Jenny

One day, my little girl Bella, who was about four at the time, set out on her bike to ride through a nature trail for the first time without training wheels. As she got to the top of a sizable hill, her eyes widened with excitement as she witnessed the bigger girls fly down before her, squealing in delight.

Just as she was about to lift her foot onto the pedal, a few women approached her, one remarking, "Oh dear, you're going down that big and scary hill on your bike are you? Be careful!" Bella's expression quickly turned from excitement to fear. Her feet turned from being buoyant feathers to heavy weights, which were now anchored to the ground. She went from seeing adventure and fun at the top of that hill to being consumed by dread and doubt.

It took a great deal of convincing that she indeed had everything inside of her to take on that hill successfully. After much encouragement, she finally lifted her feet and gave in to trusting her abilities. When she landed at the bottom, she looked up with a glowing expression of joy from her achievement, knowing she'd overcome not only her own fears but the fears of those around her.

How do you begin to live an internally referenced life? Turn up the volume on our inner voice of truth (what Dr. Christiane Northrup calls the inner guidance system) and turn down the volume on the outside voices that can guide us in directions that aren't always aligned with our deepest desires.

Bhoga versus Yoga

In Western culture, we are taught that money, brand names, fancy clothing and jewelry are the important measurements by which we should live our lives. We are encouraged to compare ourselves, and when we do, we inevitably find ourselves inadequately measuring up to the unrealistic images in the media.

This externally focused attitude is what the ancient sages called **Bhoga** (sounds a lot like bogus, doesn't it?), which refers to the unconscious pattern of living for sensory pleasure. Living in such a way lures us into the mall or to the plastic surgeon's office, putting us in debt or in pain, which disempowers us even more than when we started. It may appear to be cool to hang out at the mall and wear the top seasonal fashions, but if it's putting you or your family in debt, that's a very unskillful way of living life. As activist and author Sophia Amoruso said, "Your money looks better in the bank than it does on your feet." [13]

Here's a truth about life: there will always be someone better and seemingly more beautiful than you, and there will always be someone less capable than you. The best approach to building confidence and the happiness that follows is to stop comparing and competing with others, and to gaze, instead, inside and recognize your true gifts. When you can identify your natural talents and passions, you've taken the first step on the road to living confidently as a Girl on Fire. What makes you work for hours on end without notice of the time? Babysitting? Graphic design? Woodworking? Helping others? Music? Art? Gardening? Sport?

Let's explore what's its like to live an internally referenced life. A woman who is peaceful, content, confident and accepts herself as she is in the moment has definitely learned to live from the inside out, which the ancients called Yoga. A woman who is self-sustained and content with herself doesn't share the same desperate need to consume things as the woman who is reliant on the outside world for inner validation. Since her bucket is already full, she doesn't need to incessantly fill it with material items in order to affirm her existence. She is cool being who she is; imperfectly, perfectly her.

From this viewpoint, which type of woman does the consumer world depend on for revenue? The path of Bhoga, of course.

Does it make sense then that many marketing campaigns are actually designed to make us feel inadequate, so that they can present this mascara or that brand name as the answer to our insecurity?

Women want to be seen for who they really are, which is not a brand name, but a force to be reckoned with. How do you want to be seen or recognized in the world? Is there a legacy you'd like to leave behind after you've died?

---

[13] Anne Kingston, "New Girl, Go Girl", MacLean's Magazine, September 27, 2014, http://www.macleans.ca/society/new-girl-go-girl/

Take a moment to reflect on a recent decision you've made in your life. Was it based on living from the outside in (in an externally referenced way) or from the inside out (in an internally referenced way)? Did you listen to the outer voices or listen to your loving, inner voice?

Note: Remember we all have two inner voices: a lover and a critic. Living in a self-referred way means that we listen to the voice of love and respect within, not the inner critic which is just an echo of the outside voices telling us we're not good enough.

THE BEAUTY MYTH

Society has attempted to diminish women to being "sexy." But there is so much more to being a woman than our sex appeal, in fact, that is the least of our assets!

Confining women to the role of a perfectly looking, sexual being, prevents us from fully expressing our true potential and sharing our greatest gifts. What's more, beauty in the way it's idolized today, has an expiry date. So what will you rely on when your face starts to wrinkle and your breasts start to sag, when your thighs dimple and your upper arms jiggle? We must develop our enduring female capacities within that are not temporary and dependent on the fads of society. If we do not develop lasting strengths, when our beauty changes as we age, so will our self-identity, and that's a recipe for disaster.

Do you really want to spend your life obsessed with your clothing, hair and make up? Or do you want to develop your natural gifts that will inevitably uplift your community and contribute to the betterment of the world?

If you think your sexy outfit gives you a winning advantage, think again.

Barbara Frederickson conducted a very intriguing study in which she randomly chose girls and guys to dress up in either a loose sweater or a swimsuit and complete a quiz. With no observers and no windows, the results showed that the men in a swimsuit did marginally better than the others wearing the sweater. The girls however, performed significantly worse when wearing the full piece suit than those wearing the bulky sweater. And it's a safe bet to say that the girls wearing the suits would have performed even more poorly in a classroom of peers. The researchers called this self-objectification, where girls grew to view their bodies as objects to be evaluated and rated. Leonard Sax claims that when a teen girl goes to school wearing revealing outfits, "she's going to be thinking about, analyzing and judging her own body when she ought to be thinking about geometry or Spanish grammar."[14]

Really now, if sex appeal and outer beauty were the answers to our longing for lasting happiness, we wouldn't see iconic stars, such as Marilyn Monroe, battle with depression and succumb to drug overdoses. Even 50 years since her death, Marilyn is still considered one of the world's most renowned sex symbols of our time. If we were to believe in the media's promise that beauty and sex appeal bring happiness, then, why did Marilyn make remarks such as "Sometimes I feel my whole life has been one big rejection," and "When you feel beaten inside, you don't feel angry at those who have beaten you. You just feel ashamed." If sex appeal didn't bring happiness for Marilyn, why do we believe that it will solve our problems?

---

14 Leonard Sax, Girls On The Edge, (Basic Books, 2011), 28.

Unfortunately, Marilyn is a reflection of what research is discovering today in that sexual objectification diminishes women's self-worth and self-esteem by holding them to a standard of perfection and treating them as objects of temporary pleasure.

Perhaps if Marilyn had cultivated a few of the inner treasures we're exploring, her life might have taken a different path and would have lasted beyond just 36 short years.

Are you seeking the conditional approval of society and longing to fit in?

Some cultural beliefs around thin being better and more beautiful than larger bodies:

- The average American woman is 5'4" tall and weighs 165 pounds. The average Miss America winner is 5'7" and weighs 121 pounds.[15]
- The average BMI of Miss America winners has decreased from around 22 in the 1920s to 16.9 in the 2000s. The World Health Organization classifies a normal BMI as falling between 18.5 and 24.9 [16]
- Of American elementary school girls who read magazines, 69% say that the pictures influence their concept of the ideal body shape. 47% say the pictures make them want to lose weight[17]
- 81% of 10 year olds are afraid of being fat[18]

Self-punishment

Women of all ages across the world are "busting their butts" to fulfill the preconceived notions of what it means to be a woman today. Being fully human does NOT require us to punish ourselves on a regular basis.

What does it mean to you to be a woman in the world today?

Ultimately, what everybody is searching for in life is the experience of being loved for who they are. What so many women don't realize is that this unconditional love doesn't come with the price tag we've put on it. Many of us believe that we have to tough it out and push ourselves to the limit in all aspects of our life, including work, school, fitness, beauty and caregiving, in order to be worthy of receiving love. But when we constantly push ourselves past our limits, we only deplete our store of life energy, leading to depression, fatigue, hopelessness and illness.

Instead of tapping out our energy reserve each day, in an attempt to feel okay about ourselves, what if we took the approach of listening to what brings us joy and nourishment? What if we replaced the grueling uphill run that depletes our energy with a nourishing yoga class that heals our body and soul? Life doesn't have to be a series of one punishing activity after another. You are not here to abuse yourself. Life is tough enough outside the walls of your own skin!

---

[15] "Get the Facts on Eating disorders", NEDA Feeding Hope, accessed September 2016, https://www.nationaleatingdisorders.org/get-facts-eating-disorders
[16] Ibid.
[17] Ibid.
[18] Ibid.

What are some of the societal pressures and expectations that you have, up to this point, assumed are normal? Have you learned that life is a lot of hard work and not much fun? Have you learned that you need to override your body's needs or your deeper soul desires in order to be someone in the world? If so, how has that affected your confidence in yourself?

Cultivating Confidence

Henry David Thoreau once said "Move confidently in the direction of your dreams! Live the life you've imagined."

If you wait for the world around you to give you permission to claim your confidence, you'll be waiting your whole life. Life can be tough, people can be mean. Whatever beliefs you hold about yourself will be mirrored out to the world and reflected back to you in the people around you. In other words, if you lack confidence in yourself (within your internal environment), the people around you (your external environment) will reflect that back by treating you poorly, as a person who is not worthy of respect.

The moment you alter your internal environment and declare that you are worthy of respect and commit to boosting your confidence, amazing things will happen. Your outer world will reflect that self-love and confidence, and you'll notice people treating you differently, more respectfully. With greater and greater confidence, you'll naturally attract caring friends, you'll attract people who really want to hear what you have to say and you'll draw to you, opportunities that harmonize with your heart's desires.

As we begin our journey of self-inquiry for greater understanding of who we are, it is very helpful to do some personal research on past generations to discover what challenges they faced and how they dealt with them. It is important to understand that behavioral patterns and personality traits are often passed down in our genetic make up. We not only inherit the helpful traits of ancestors, like grit and perseverance, but we can also inherit the emotional trauma that was left unhealed (and much of our ancestors' issues were left unhealed as they didn't have the luxury of time and resources to effectively deal with them, as we do).

If you struggle with low self-esteem or lack of confidence, it is very likely that there is a family history of this emotional pattern from past generations. The good news is that we can re-invent our lives, at any time, with the gift of self awareness and personal choice. After all, our job in this lifetime is to learn from past mistakes and use those lessons to help us grow so that we one day surpass the level of consciousness of previous generations. If we all did this, the human species would improve immensely over time.

Girl on Fire Poem

The Girl on fire is the wild woman who burns
through her contract with mediocrity
with the flame in her heart.
She releases herself from outmoded ways of being
and liberates herself from the pain of the past,
transforming into a new, radiant version of herself.

This Girl on Fire obeys the powerful energy of her heart fire,
which sparks her inner flame of passion,
inspiring her to express her true essence and live
at a love frequency that heals all.

The power of transformation lives
within the flame of your heart.
Starting today, begin to peel away the layers
that veil your inner radiance so that one day
there will nothing in the way
of you sharing your own beautiful light with the world!

Omwork

Visit the mall and spend 30 minutes observing the messages within the images of women. What is the marketing attempting to convey? Also notice what females of all ages are wearing. Do they look content, happy, confident, at peace? Record your observations to both questions.

Also, go home and decorate your scales, pasting images of women who are changing the world with their inner flame. Instead of using your scales to weigh yourself and determine your self-esteem each day, use them as art to inspire you to step into the real game of life and contribute positively.

List three successes you've had in the last six months (if you can't come up with three, keep digging, they are there):

1. _____
2. _____
3. _____

Positive experiences and personal successes fuel our confidence. Go ahead and list three achievements you intend to accomplish over the next six months (be reasonable enough that you set yourself up for success but be wild enough to give yourself a challenge):

1. _____
2. _____
3. _____

Affirmation

I am free to connect to and live from the center of power within me, which is a reflection of my true self.

When I am centered in my own source of power, I am unaffected by the false glitter that surrounds me.

Our work is to find out who we are, and then choose to love ourselves, as we are, as we grow.

I gracefully cope with criticism by dialing into my core of self-worth and turning up the volume on my positive inner dialogue.

Personal additions:

Physical Posture

Mountain Pose

Additional Omwork Reading - Sleep

The teen years typically require about 10-12 hours of sleep a night. Most teens skimp on sleep throughout the week and spend the weekend attempting to catch up. A good night's sleep is an essential component of *swasthi*/health and is necessary to keep the inner flame aglow.

According to Frances E. Jenson, author of the Teenage Brain, sleep patterns change throughout our lives. She calls infants and children "larks" as they wake up early and go to sleep early. She then calls adolescents "owls," because they stay up late and sleep in in the morning. As we approach adulthood, we tend to revert back to the early to bed, early to rise pattern.

The schedule we've culturally created for teens demands that they abide by our adult circadian rhythm, by rising early for school and work. But this early morning start apparently doesn't translate into an early night, as the teen brain tends to hold that part of the pattern.

What does that equate to? Exactly what we see in teens today: a chronically sleep deprived teenage population. The typical teenage body operates optimally on 9-10hrs of sleep per night and most teens today are getting a mere 6-8hrs.

Jensen claims that sleep deprivation causes more than just physical fatigue. It can contribute to juvenile delinquency, criminal behavior, depression, obesity, high blood pressure, cardiovascular disease. [19]It also leads teens to consume more soft drinks, fried food, sweets and caffeine. Additionally, it leads to more screen time (which diminishes much needed melatonin), increased TV watching, less activity and higher rates of suicide.

Did you know that sleep integrates our learning from the day before, feeds our memory, helps us eat better, manage stress more effectively and improves athletic performance?

Signs of sleep deprivation

- Fatigued throughout the day, especially mid afternoon
- Inability to concentrate clearly
- Dependence on a stimulant, such as caffeine, to successfully complete daily tasks
- Unexplained weight gain

Helpful hints for getting a good night sleep

- Avoid consuming heavy food past 7 pm
- Step away from the screen in the evening to restore your optic nerve and melatonin.
- Remove all technological devices from your sleeping area and train your body to wake up naturally without an alarm. Set the intention to awake at the time your alarm goes off and soon your body will do it automatically. If using an alarm, have it turned on to uplifting, soft music to ease you into wakefulness
- Feather your nest by creating a comforting and cozy sleeping environment
- Be prepared and organized for the morning so you can relax into the moment
- Right before you sleep is a great time to daydream. The last thing you think about is what you'll take into your dream world, so consciously create images or visions that will uplift your nighttime experience and bring you closer to your life vision
- Fill your nighttime routine with gentleness, beauty and *sattvic*/peaceful influences, such as reading by candle light, or gentle movement to soft music. Slow asanas will help you to deepen and slow down your breathing, leading to a relaxed body state
- Meditation calms and clears the mind of worry and overthinking. Affirm to yourself when worry arises, "This thought does not belong here"
- If your energy needs calming, sleepytime and camomile teas are very effective. GABBA is a natural anti-anxiety supplement but should be approved by your doctor first if you are taking medication
- A darkened room will help the release of melatonin, an essential hormone that repairs tissue and heals the body
- If you're having issues sleeping, you could also consult with your doctor.
- Take a moment before you rise to set your highest intention for the day, how do you want to feel (self-worth)? How you do you want to show up in the world (self-esteem)? Whose life can you enhance through your presence (contribution)?

---

[19] Frances E. Jensen, *The Teenage Brain*, (Colins, Jan 2015), 96

- Upon waking, stretch, relax and count your blessings. Recall your daydream of your deepest desires for your life and imagine stepping into that vision as you rise

What else could you add to this list of suggestions? Is there anything you do that works in helping you sleep?

Mindful Movement Class - Week 4

NOTE: This is the Mindful Movement Class to accompany Week 4. For consistency and ease, we recommend the video series of these classes available at www.GirlOnFire.ca.

Weekly theme – Confidence
Mountain Pose/Bamboo Pose   Gather and Ground   Fire Breathing   Shoulder shrugs and arm circles   Windmill   Prana Pull Flow   Standing Half Moon Pose   **Feature Posture:** Mountain Pose/Bamboo Pose   Classical Namaskaras   Warrior 1 with eagle arms into Warrior 3.   Warrior Squats   Quad stretch to Bow   **Partner Posture:** Bow Assist   Table with undulating spine   Child's Pose   Supine Twist   Cat Tail Pose   Savasana/Relaxation Pose
Girl on Fire closing   To acknowledge the three centers of Power, Love and Insight: Rise to sitting and bring palms together. Lift hands so that thumbs touch the mid eye point and say: *"Guided by insight"*   Now draw hands to heart, one palm on heart center in the middle of the chest and the other palm resting on top of the first hand and say: *"I listen to my heart's desire"*   Now take the top hand and slide it down so it rests on the navel, with the first hand remaining on the heart and say: *"And take positive, powerful action in the world"*

NOTES

Week 5 – Discernment

This week's focus is to gain deeper understanding of:
- Training the Brain with BREATH
- The path of behavior change
- Romance and rose colored glasses
- Establishing Healthy Boundaries

Discernment is the ability to see and understand people, things, or situations clearly and intelligently.

As simple as this may sound, developing discernment requires a great deal of inner work because we must move through the veil of illusion and emotional upheaval to see the world as it is, which very few people fully achieve. Most of us have developed beliefs about almost everything we see and experience around us. When we hear the word chair, we all have an idea and image that comes to mind about what a chair is that's based on our experience of it and what we've been told about it. This is called conditioning. Learning to see clearly begins with the realization that we have a unique (and often small) perspective based on our life experience. This allows us to have more compassion for ourselves and others.

A MESSAGE FROM JENNY

According to yogic wisdom, discernment is the result of combined effort of the mind, heart and gut instinct. When all of these aspects of our being are working together, we can fully exercise discernment and make decisions that align with our beliefs, our feelings and our deepest values.

Discernment is a very important quality for women to have. It's so important that movie after movie has been themed after it. Take Frozen for example. Doesn't Anna start out impulsive and gullible with a childlike innocence? And eventually, she matures into a discerning, strong young woman. This is our journey, too. It is filled with heartache, disillusionment and eventually intuitive wisdom and discernment.

Personally speaking, discernment has been one of my greatest challenges. I grew up with a mother who was taught when she was young to be polite and kind to everyone. Although a very altruistic approach to life, it has a few major pitfalls. For example, that system's okay if everyone is being polite and kind in return, but what if someone is threatening or undermining your well being? Feeling trapped in a paradigm of having to be nice and polite, this way of relating to people forced me to put others' needs before mine.

In my twenties I began to deeply question this way of being, as I realized I was compromising my own safety and comfort with my compulsive concern with being perceived as sweet and agreeable. Then I attended a workshop by a spiritual teacher who was a little rough around the edges. His message, delivered in clear and simple language, struck a deep chord and rang through me as if saying, "This is a strange new truth that will save your life, pay attention!"

The gist of his message was based on what he called the law of lesser pissers. Funny, hey? His law of lesser pissers claimed that in a difficult situation, you could choose to please the other person and compromise your own needs, which would likely leave a deep imprint on your life for months or maybe even years. The other option is that you choose to use discernment and honor your own intuitive wisdom by setting boundaries that respect your needs even at the risk of pissing off the other person. This might last a few minutes, maybe a little more. Over all, which scenario leaves the most damage? The first one of course, when we compromise ourselves to please another. According to the law of lesser pissers, it might be uncomfortable in the moment to stand for your own well-being, but they'll get over it. You on the other hand, could inflict harm on yourself by disrespecting your needs and potentially leave an indelible mark on your soul.

A few months after hearing this, I met a man who invited me out for a joyride on his motorbike. I had grown up with an older brother who rode bikes and he was always very strict about wearing proper protective gear. I didn't know this guy very well, and I was leery of his road safety, especially when he showed up in shorts and a t-shirt (not the standard leather outfit and boots I was accustomed to seeing). Had I known the BREATH method, I would have paused, checked in with myself and noticed the pain in my gut screaming for me to walk away.

Unfortunately, I was so entrenched in the need to please pattern, that I tucked my hair into the helmet and jumped on the back. He accelerated so fast out of the parking lot that he almost lost me off the back within the first few seconds of our joyride. After an agonizing ocean view ride of weaving in and out of cars and hugging tight corners, we finally returned to my car with a jarring stop. While I stumbled off the bike, shaking from the one too many close calls, he sat back grinning from ear to ear, seemingly pleased to have survived another brush with death.

I consider myself lucky to have walked away from that experience with a chance to next time, breathe, listen and act in accordance with my inner guidance system. Even though that event shook me to the core and taught me important lessons, there have been a number of times since then that I've made choices that weren't aligned with my highest good. But each time I've fallen into the hole, I've grown and strengthened my discernment muscle, which has allowed me to step off the people-pleasing path and step onto discernment drive. While some may view this shift as being selfish, it is an essential one for taking care of yourself.

Growth isn't always instantaneous, and you may call yourself a slow learner, but the point is you're learning.

Jenny

Training the brain with BREATH

The practice of yoga teaches us to fully experience the present moment. Why do we want to do that? Because our lives are a compilation of moments, and many of us skip through life because we're distracted, or lacking the tools to deal with life's challenges. To be right here in this moment without dreaming about the future or reminiscing over the past, requires both discipline and courage. Discipline because the fantasy world can be so much more compelling than the not so perfect present moment and courage because sometimes staying in the present moment is a tough place to be. As a Girl on Fire, you are learning to effectively deal with life's peaks and valleys, while maintaining a steady inner flame of well-being. When we step outside of the stream of wellbeing, it's more difficult to access our discernment and make healthy choices in our lives. When we are in balance, and present in the moment, discernment is way more accessible. There is a simple structure that we can follow to help us stay present to life as it arises.

Our lives are unfolding at a such a rapid pace today that many of us just move from one event to another, without fully experiencing the moment, or missing the lessons available to us. We are like professional buffet consumers, rushing from one feast to another, eating our next meal before the previous one is digested. This BREATH process creates the necessary space we need to land in the now and to fully experience the moment and digest its flavors and nutrients in order to grow from our life experiences and learn the lessons at hand.

What's more, we make our wisest and most self-respecting choices when we're able to access our reasoning mind, which is available to us when we feel calm and relaxed. Alternatively, it's when we're in a state of panic or reactivity that we often do and say things that we otherwise would never consider because we're operating from the state of fight or flight. Therefore, this BREATH process is helpful in creating the much needed pause, especially for the impulsive nature of the teenage brain, to calm down and tap our discernment potential. Sometimes all it takes is a few deep slow breaths away from a trigger to sink into the wise, calm and clear you.

Here is the BREATH structure to help you do that:

Step 1: Breathe

A few, deep, full breaths provide us with a pause, which can change our whole perspective. When we follow the stress response, we can literally lose our mind and succumb to panic. But when we're able to stay present to our breath, we have a better shot at staying calm and rational, breaking the loop of obsessive thinking and negative emotional addictions. Instead of starting with the inhalation, as most of us do when we think to breathe, try exhaling first. This aspect of the breath activates the rest and digest part of our nervous system, reminding us to soften into the moment. This is the first step in returning home to ourselves.

STEP 2: RELAX

Once we've located our breath, we can guide the breath through the body to scan for areas of tension and consciously begin to relax and let go. Sometimes we become anxious first and then tense the body, but other times habitual tension itself can create uneasiness that sends us into fight or flight. Conscious relaxation establishes us in the desired state of restful awareness.

STEP 3: EXPERIENCE

Our bodies are constantly communicating to us, and it's amazing how many messages and warning signs we catch when we start to tune in. To actually feel what's going on inside requires us to pay attention to the energy and sensation within our bodies, with a fresh and curious perspective. Fully experiencing the moment reveals information within our bodies (and our lives) that we've otherwise ignored.

STEP 4: ALLOW

This step requires us to a) relinquish our need for control and b) let go of any expectations for a specific outcome. The nature of allowing encourages us to lift the anchor and let our boat float downstream, which makes space for healing, growth and delight. Can you hear how this step of allowing life to just be as it is, calls us to apply the qualities of ease and effortlessness?

STEP 5: TEND TO THE MOMENT

This step calls us to activate the wisest part of our minds, the part that tends to the moment and observes life. Here we simply witness the unfolding of the moment without judgment or criticism. When we learn to truly observe what's happening, we can experience life's challenges without becoming consumed by drama. When we tend to the moment, we can linger in the eye of the storm without being blown off our center. It is this part of our awareness that reminds us to breathe, relax and experience life in all its fullness.

STEP 6: HEALTH

By practicing this approach to life, we pull ourselves out of the fight or flight cycle of reactivity into the domain of discernment and wisdom, both of which lie within present moment awareness. It is at this point in the process where we take lessons from our current life experience, and move forward into the next juicy adventure of life with a healthy, integrated attitude.

Reflection

Placing your hands on your chest, gently circle your hands. As you breathe deeply and smoothly, let this posture heal your body and your heart, healing any ways that your boundaries have been violated in the past by others, or by you. Imagine white light entering your heart space, freeing you of pain, resentment or shame. Let those emotions be transformed into forgiveness, love, self-respect and peace.

> Between stimulus and response, there is a space. In that space is our power to choose our response. In our response lies our growth and our freedom. ~ Victor Frankl

The Path of Behavior Change

Discernment can help us make life-giving, fire-fueling decisions in our lives. For example, as we learn to identify the signs of unhealthy behavior, we are able to steer clear of abusive relationships by inviting people who are worthy of our friendship into our inner circle. If proper discernment was not modeled to you during childhood, it may take years to cultivate, but it's one of those inner treasures that will save you much heartache and pain.

On the path to discernment, it is essential that we accept that mistakes will be made along the way. The question is: how will you treat yourself when you make choices that don't align with your intentions to be self-loving and respectful? Will you beat yourself up and employ your self-critic? Or will you compassionately hold space for yourself as a human being, who is a work in progress? Will you reflect on the factors that led you to make the choices you made with an attitude of curiosity and dedication to growth?

There is a poignant analogy written for Alcoholics Anonymous that describes this process nicely.

Phase 1: disorientation

Imagine yourself walking down the road and, all of a sudden, you're in total darkness. You have no idea where you are, or how you got there. After a day or so, you realize you've fallen into a deep hole and it takes you another day to climb out. Disorientated, you slowly get up and dust yourself off. This phase is wrought with the pain and suffering that often accompanies unconscious behavior. Have you experienced this type of fall in your life, perhaps in the misuse of substances, or sexuality or peer pressure?

Phase 2: initial recognition

Now imagine yourself walking down the road again, and all of a sudden you fall into the hole again. This time is slightly different than the last because you recognize the hole and have a clue how to get out of it. Although you're disoriented and it takes you a little time to find your bearings, you're out of the hole in half the time. There is still much pain and suffering, but a shorter duration, as the seed of discernment takes root.

Phase 3: familiar recognition

Next time, you're walking down the same street, you fall into the hole and know exactly where you are and what you've done. You quickly jump out, dust yourself off and carry on with little time wasted. There is much less pain and suffering here as discernment continues to develop.

Phase 4: avoidance

The next time you're walking down the same street, you actually notice the hole in advance and walk around it. Pain and suffering are now replaced with the excitement and hope that positive behavior change brings.

Phase 5: a new path

And finally, you become so aware of your blinding pattern of darkness that you choose to take a different route altogether! This final phase of transforming the unconscious to the conscious represents the embodiment of discernment.

Can you see how much patience and compassion is required when making changes in our lives? Can you also see that over time, it's entirely possible?

Reflect on a time in your life when you chose to change a habit, or even had the desire to do so.

Were you patient with yourself, knowing that habits take time to transform?
What worked?
What didn't so much?
How might you approach a habit pattern today, keeping the process above in mind?

Romance and rose colored glasses

> The brain is a magnificent organ; it starts from the moment you're born and doesn't stop until you fall in love. [20]

Have you ever fallen so deeply in love with someone that you literally lost your mind? No matter how hard you tried to focus your thoughts, you'd inevitably slide into a dreamy fantasy of your future together? And you had difficulty finding words to communicate like a normal person in their presence? And you felt high on some crazy love potion that left you permanently grinning?

---

[20] Pat Love, quoted in Rokelle Lerner, "The Object of My Affection Is in my Reflection" (Heath Communications, 2009), 112.

According to Dr. Earl Henslin, author of *This is your brain in Love*, this crazy addictive state often accompanies the initial phase of a romantic relationship. Many call it the romance phase. And while it's intoxicating and euphoric, it can also create the emotional upheaval that often goes along with the first waves of romantic attraction: panic, anxiety, manic behavior, uneasiness, depression and obsession.

Although this may feel amazing in the moment, it can also be very hazardous because it fogs up your sense of reasoning and discernment. If you've chosen a person who is worthy of your love, you're okay. But not everyone is safe to bring into your inner circle and share your heart (and/or body) with.

When the emotional center of the brain (the limbic system) highjacks our reasoning center of the brain (the frontal cortex), we are under the influence of blissful love hormones that are equivalent to the effects of cocaine. When such passionate fire is ignited and love hormones are flowing, we might find ourselves in a relationship that doesn't have enduring qualities for a healthy long-term connection.

This is something to be particularly cautious of at times in your life when you are depressed, grieving, stressed or feeling socially isolated. The love potion, (or more specifically, dopamine) may seem like the perfect answer to your blue mood, but it's also the time when we are most vulnerable, which may cause us to allow certain people into our lives that we would otherwise never let in if we were in a healthier frame of mind.

Now that you are aware of this hormone-induced state, what are some structures you could set up in your life to protect yourself from the potential of engaging with someone who is not aligned with your highest visions for an intimate relationship?

Possible answers:
- Have a few trusted friends ready to offer their opinions
- Research the person's history and family circle to ensure they come from a family with values that match yours
- Consult a facilitator or adult mentor before taking steps toward intimate connection
- Apply the BREATH technique to help keep you calmly connected to your gut instinct and intuition

Establishing healthy boundaries

The facts: one in four girls and one in six boys world-wide are sexually violated at some point in their lives.

Porn industry revenues exceed the combined revenues of the big media companies, including ABC, CBS and NBC. Over half of all spending on the internet is related to sex.

This industry is consuming a great deal of people's time, energy and money, and sadly, is a very dysfunctional perspective of the potential of our human sexuality. Sexuality at its lowest is demonstrated in pornography-- there is no exchange of love, and often very little respect. Sexuality at its highest involves an exchange of love, appreciation, respect and generosity. While there's no judgment about how you conduct yourself sexually, we do care about how you feel before, during and after the exchange.

In his book, *Girls on the Edge*, Leonard Sax says that depression is the new STD because girls are compromising their personal boundaries and becoming sexually active because of peer pressure and other reasons. Bottom line: it feels awful when we cross our own boundaries and dishonor our inner sense of what feels good and right.

> When you say 'yes' to others, make sure you are not saying 'no' to yourself. ~ Paulo Coelho

When we transition from child to adult, from having most of our needs met within the family unit to spending most of our time with peers, decisions are no longer made for you, and you are called to be responsible for your own well-being and care.

When we reach the teenage years, peer connection becomes the most important influence. Unfortunately, the teen culture is not always a safe and loving place to be, as many teens can be quite cruel and ruthless in attempts to feel acceptable and belonging. Teens today are careless with each other's hearts. But it is possible to be hormonal and still be respectful and compassionate, toward ourselves and others.

Many young women are taught that setting appropriate and self-respecting boundaries is impolite to others. This creates a scenario where others' needs are perceived as more important than our own, reflecting low self-love and respect. When we don't put our needs at the top of our list of priorities, we become susceptible to a variety of issues such as anxiety, insecurity, addictive and compulsive disorders, fatigue and attraction to boundary crashers.

If we are to grow up and be Girl's on Fire with well cared for inner flames, we must have the skills to protect ourselves from the energies of the world. When we learn to skilfully set clear boundaries, we will start to feel safe and comfortable and begin to truly love the skin we're in. As the saying goes: self-care is an inside job!

This requires awareness of what our needs are and discernment/critical thinking in order to make wise choices. You will indeed make mistakes and when you cross your own inner boundary you'll feel it. But mistakes teach us where our edge is, and our work is to learn the first time so we don't repeat the violation. If we don't respect our boundaries, we'll continue to injure ourselves unintentionally, which can take years to heal.

You may be questioning that statement 'years to heal'? Really? Yes, because women and men are designed very differently. At a biological level, men are designed with a penis that is exterior of their body. Hormonally, they are designed to have a one time fling, insert their sperm into the woman's egg for the sake of reproduction and then move on. They are wired to impregnate as many female eggs as possible so that their DNA will continue on. This enables men to hook up with someone once, move on and not think twice about it. Men are also aroused by visual stimulation, which explains their attraction to pornography more so than women. They can keep their emotions out of the experience so that it remains strictly physical.

Teenage boys may feel like they're at the mercy of testosterone, the sex hormone that rages through their systems during adolescence. That does not give anyone permission to be aggressive or violent, but many boys are given this message. Boys are taught to fight, shoot, and be tough, emotionless beings. Life is not easy for them either. They are given many conflicting messages by society as they are (hopefully) taught to behave respectfully, but then are exposed to massive amounts of violence and sexual exploitation through various mediums.

Women on the other hand, are designed to receive and nurture. Our reproductive organs are built into our anatomy, with our womb and ovaries housed within the pelvis. When we have sex, we not only receive the man's fluid, but also his energy and his life experiences. Once the woman has had sex, hormones are released within her that drive her to want to nurture, protect and covet her new life partner. Pornography tends not to interest women as much because our pleasure comes more from acts of love, and intimate emotional connection. Our culture has unfortunately replaced sacred, loving sexual contact with pornography, and that can have long-lasting detrimental effects on our self-worth, intimacy and our sense of joy.

Imagine if all women were to refuse to be mistreated and demanded that they be treated with equal respect. Society, and the pornography industry, would need to change. With the rights and opportunities women have today, we can do this. We must pave the way.

With regards to promiscuity, it's important to be really honest with yourself about why you're having sex—for the enjoyment? For the longing to be loved? Or for a mutually beneficial intimate exchange? If you're engaging in sex because of poor boundaries or a desire to be loved, or a dire need for attention, the interactions may be detrimental to your wellbeing. It's essential that before you engage sexually with anyone that you get clear on why you're doing it and what you need from the exchange. Then you can communicate that and hold to it. Awareness is the golden key, and it begins with self-inquiry. That means asking questions about why you do the things you do.

Our first experience of physical touch comes from our immediate family. Touch is essential to our health, as we know that babies who are bereft of physical contact are actually at risk of dying. As children we engaged in physical contact with friends through games and body play. As teens, we are inundated with new surges of hormones that lead to the beginning of sexual exploration.

The quality of the touch we receive as children can determine what we accept as normal when we become teens and adults. Whatever we accept as normal within relationships is what we'll welcome into our lives.

Many of us were not given permission, or encouraged to set clear physical boundaries, as we were told that to do so was rude, impolite or not allowed. Can you think of an example where you were socially expected to override your instinct to protect or withdraw from someone?

DISCUSSION TIME OR INNER REFLECTION

Our physical energetic boundaries serve to protect us from harmful energy. When we are in the presence of loving contact, our boundaries can dissolve, allowing us to fully experience human connection. Your boundaries will operate in this way if you had healthy touch as a child, if you were lovingly cuddled and cared for tenderly when the need arose.

Your boundaries might not work as effectively if you were touched inappropriately or violated in some way. As teens and adults, you may be at risk of attracting the same hurtful contact and you might even push away healthy interaction, or all interaction period, which can lead to depression and isolation. Our challenge then is to heal past harmful experiences in order to attract loving, respectful interactions.

When your partner is healthy and respectful, positive energy is exchanged. But if your partner has unhealthy lifestyle habits, such as addiction, or abusive/violent tendencies, that energy will be transmitted into your system, leaving a deep imprint on your system.

And very important is the essential conversation about pregnancy and STD's (sexually transmitted diseases) and STI's (sexually transmitted infections), which is difficult to have in the heat of the moment. Many teens engage sexually when they are under the influence of drugs or alcohol, which is very hazardous, even life threatening. As hard as it is for teens to think beyond the moment, it is crucial to realize that the choices you make, either actively by saying 'yes' or passively by not expressing your boundaries, often have irreversible results. It only takes one interaction to contract an STD or STI that you must live with for the rest of your life. STD's are not just contracted through intercourse, but also through oral contact as well.

To protect yourself from the possibility of contracting an STD or STI, it is recommended to abstain from contact until you and your partner have been thoroughly tested, even if you're symptom free. Many STI's go unrecognized because they have no symptoms. And a long term monogamous relationship is always the best course of action.

In her book, **Energetic Boundaries**, Cyndi Dale refers to a study from the Kinsey Institute. According to their research, 18-29 year olds have sex about 112 times a year. If we have sex 2/week, we'll end up having about 5,000 sexual acts in our lifetime. That's a lot of sexual-energetic exchanges!

If we are affected by all of our lifestyle habits, including and especially our relationship interactions, we must pause and consider the impact of our sexual interactions on our health.

Are your sexual interactions nourishing?

Do they contribute to your wellbeing or are they draining your health and contributing to your toxic load?

This is an important conversation for us to have at an early age so that we can navigate ourselves through this time of exploration with awareness of the impact of our actions on our long term health and self-respect.

We as young women cannot rely on anyone else to affirm our existence. Instead of seeking acceptance and love from outside sources, we must retrieve our sense of self and return it to its rightful place within us, as it is the very core of who we are. We must reclaim our flame!

What are some qualities that describe healthy sexual exchanges?

Respect, tenderness, love, eagerness to give and receive, etc.

What are your hopes and intentions for your future sexual relationships?

Do you give yourself permission to set appropriate, healthy boundaries?

Can you forgive yourself for any interactions you've had in the past that weren't loving and respectful?

Have you considered self pleasure to familiarize yourself with your body's likes and dislikes? Masturbation is an ideal way to explore your sexuality in a safe, pleasurable way that removes you from becoming intertwined in the emotional web that so often accompanies sexual exchanges.

Above all, you must nurture your self-respect and self-esteem. Low self-esteem can be the greatest threat to your wellbeing because you are the one who must now care for yourself by setting proper boundaries.

Optional Craft: Body paint around the navel (2nd chakra) drawing words and symbols that reflect healthy energetic boundaries.

Yoni mudra with hands on lower abdomen. **Yoni is the Sanskrit term for womb, encompassing our whole region of sexuality in the second chakra. It translates into "the source of the sacred"** or "the sacred space." Imagine if all women treated their bodies as though they were the source of all that is sacred and special in the world?

Omwork

A call to make a change

When we're outside of the stream of well-being, caused by either physical or mental misalignment, it's not bad or good. Without judgment, we can view this state of misalignment as a call to use discernment and refine our lifestyle habits accordingly.

Begin with the BREATH process and then take a few moments to journal about a habit or behavior in your life that you would like to transform using the wisdom of discernment. If nothing specific comes to mind, it may be helpful to generally assess your life, and your approach to it, including your schedule, work, school, friends, stress levels, thoughts and inner dialogue.

In terms of this current habit, what phase are you living in, with regards to the **path of behavior change**?

Freely write about what it would feel like to walk around the hole and eventually choose a different route?

What would your life be like? Include as many details as possible!

Making changes to your life can be really scary. That's because doing anything we've never done before is always uncertain and lacks the control we may be used to having. But, remember, change can also be exciting and filled with possibility for improvement.

Making change requires the faith that all will be well.

Shraddha, or faith, is required for anyone on the yogic path, as we are called to surrender into the flow of life, and to listen intently to our hearts and follow the direction of our inner longings. Having faith that we are guided by a universal power allows us to let go while trusting that we are being led toward our highest good. With faith, we learn to approach life with optimism, expecting miracles and positive surprises.

What boosts your ability to have faith in the goodness of life?

Some suggestions:

Moving the body can release fear energy and instill a sense of connection to all of life

Mindful awareness of our breathing can expand our heart, bringing a deeper sense of faith in the journey

Spending time with a positive friend or mentor can redirect thoughts of doom to a perspective of hope

Read books about people, like Nelson Mandela, who have overcome great adversity through the power of their inner conviction

Engage in a personal passion that you're good at, that inspires a sense of achievement to counter feelings of self-doubt.

When we consciously choose to fill our lives with positive, faith affirming experiences, we are fueling the spark of light within, leading us toward our highest self, who is unstoppable, unbounded, free and strong.

Affirmations

With practice and patience, I am learning to see situations more clearly, which helps me to live more safely in the world.

When I say 'yes' to others, I make sure I am also saying 'yes' to myself.

I spend time with people who allow me to be myself and accept me for who I am.

I am worthy of greatness and have complete faith that good things are coming my way.

Personal additions:

Physical posture

Draw the Bow

Additional Omwork Reading

Reflections on healthy boundaries:
- Setting healthy boundaries does not mean you're selfish, it means you're self loving.
- Setting boundaries is a healthy way of taking care of your own needs; it doesn't mean you intend to harm or offend others.
- The more you can respect others boundaries, the more inclined they will be to honour yours.
- Your boundaries can change as you grow and change, they are not written in stone.
- Healthy boundaries help to cultivate and maintain healthy relationships.
- It is important to set healthy boundaries with others, as well as with yourself.
- Setting healthy boundaries involves saying 'yes' when it's appropriate and 'no' when it's necessary.

Ways of relating that harm our boundaries
- Ridicule
- Mockery
- Belittling
- Demanding conformity
- Control
- Abuse of any kind
- Neglect
- Sarcasm
- Heavy judgments
- Threats
- Do you have any additions to this list?

If your personal boundaries have been violated, you may find it difficult to distinguish between appropriate behavior and inappropriate behavior. Here is a list of boundary strengthening suggestions:

1) Listen to your inner GPS, your gut feeling or your heart's tug
2) Give yourself permission to say "NO"
3) Give yourself the freedom to say "YES" to life's goodness
4) Respect your feelings, and others' feelings
5) Seek support from professional or personal relationships
6) Respect your uniqueness
7) Encourage others to be themselves
8) Acknowledge your own needs
9) Give yourself permission to express yourself
10) Surround yourself with healthy models

Our younger years influence our worldview in profound ways for the remainder of our lives, unless we properly address these learned behaviors. Here is our chance to heal previous boundary violations and establish new and healthy ways of being in the world.

Mindful Movement Class - Week 5

NOTE: This is the Mindful Movement Class to accompany Week 5. For consistency and ease, we recommend the video series of these classes available at www.GirlOnFire.ca.

Weekly theme – Discernment
Seated Spinal Wave Neck stretches Shoulder rolls Arm vinyasa Knocking on the door of life Moon over the water, both directions Standing Half Moon with isometric stretch Breath of Joy Powerful pose to forward bend vinyasa Rag Doll Classical Namaskaras, slow and fast Mountain Pose **Feature Posture:** Draw the Bow Wide legged forward bend to Skandasana Beautiful Woman Pose into Eagle Pose Cobra 3x Bow Child's Pose **Partner Posture:** Supported Fish Pose Seated Forward Bend Savasana/Relaxation Pose Seated Centering Flow
Girl on Fire closing To acknowledge the three centers of Power, Love and Insight: Rise to sitting and bring palms together. Lift hands so that thumbs touch the mid eye point and say: *"Guided by insight"* Now draw hands to heart, one palm on heart center in the middle of the chest and the other palm resting on top of the first hand and say: *"I listen to my heart's desire"* Now take the top hand and slide it down so it rests on the navel, with the first hand remaining on the heart and say: *"And take positive, powerful action in the world"*

Notes

Week 6 – Resilience

This week's focus is to gain deeper understanding of:
- Stoking our inner fire
- Sukha and Dhuka
- Healthy Emotions and the Three A's
- Anxiety and Stress

> She who is flexible will not be bent out of shape. ~ Author unknown

There's a saying in yoga that infinite flexibility is the key to immortality. Let's expand on this statement further by exploring the qualities of a tree. How might you describe a tree that is healthy and growing well in a favorable environment? Its leaves are green and full, its root system is firmly established in the soil and its trunk is strong yet flexible. In a storm, this tree is able to sway with the wind, unharmed, because its tissues are healthy and therefore, flexible.

On the other hand, let's consider a tree that is struggling in a challenging environment. How would you describe this one? Without proper soil, its roots might be exposed, its trunk stiff and brittle and its needles yellow with malnourishment. When the same storm blows through this forest, this weakened tree is likely to uproot or break because it lacks the health that's required to withstand such challenge.

We humans are much the same. It's difficult to be flexible when we are filled with physical or emotional toxicity, making us feel dull, drained, stiff and stressed out. When we are healthy and well nourished, however, we are better equipped to deal with the occasional storm life throws our way, and we can weather the storm without losing a limb, so to speak, or our minds. This quality of flexibility is also known as resilience, which is our ability to bounce back, or more accurately, learn from life as it unfolds and bounce forward into growth.

In yoga we focus a great deal on flexibility of the body, but true flexibility, or resilience, includes our ability to mentally and emotionally ride the wave of life.

Michael Ungar from the Resilience Research Centre describes resiliency in this way:

> In the context of exposure to significant adversity, resilience is both the capacity of individuals to navigate their way to the psychological, social, cultural, and physical resources that sustain their well-being. (See also Ungar, 2008 and Ungar, 2011).

Take a few moments to practice the BREATH process from the previous lesson and then think of a time when a storm struck your life. Do you remember how you dealt with it? Did your actions lead to growth and return you to balance or did they cause harm to you or others?

With a little resilience training, we can learn self-regulation techniques that help us to manage our emotions and respond to challenge in a way that brings us back to the stream of well-being, not away from it.

Affirmation: I bend so that I don't break.

Stoking the Fire

When the previous inner treasures of self-awareness, self-worth, confidence and discernment are firmly established and we are living within the stream of well-being, we are more able to bounce back from life's experiences. When we are living out of balance, for example, depraved of sleep or love, or gripped by addiction, our system will be less likely to effectively ride the wave of challenge when it arises.

By stoking our inner fire, we become more skilled at using our life experiences, both positive and negative, as fuel for our flame.

Imagine your core as a fire pit. If your fire is well stoked and glowing brightly (as it does when we are living within the stream of well-being), it will have the power to burn good, dry wood as well as those pieces that are old, wet and moldy. Here, we are able to process positive life experiences and bounce back from the tough lessons because our core flame is strong.

Alternatively, if your inner fire pit is weak and burning poorly (as it does when we are imbalanced or deficient in our inner treasures), even the best pieces of firewood take a long time to burn, and the wet ones just dampen the flame even more. In this state, we are at risk of our flame being extinguished because the positive life experiences can't fuel us and the negative one's further destroy what little fire we have burning.

We can also have too much fire, which can be equally devastating to our well-being.

Let's take anger for example. We all know what it feels like to be consumed by anger; our eyes widen, fists clench and we usually have the impulse to push or yell to release this massive surge of intense energy. But strong, fiery emotions can be very disturbing to our system, burning away important life force energy and disrupting our inner balance.

Our job in life is to keep our inner flame, what yogis called agni, well stoked, but not too hot, through our fire fueling practices such as positivity and kindness toward ourselves and healthy lifestyle habits.

Soak in the *Sukha*, Distance the *Dukha*

We don't have the choice *not* to think, that's what the mind does, but we do have choice about what kind of thoughts we think.

In yoga, there are two opposing terms, *sukha*, which refers to ease and happiness and *dukha*, which refers to pain and suffering. Many of us have had pain and suffering hardwired into our systems. Is there a pattern of dukha you can identify in your life? You may have learned from your peers to complain, criticize, or blame. These are all very common, yet destructive modes of behavior.

Through the health-promoting practices in this program, we can make the shift from *dukha* to *sukha*.

Affirmation

Soak in the sukha, *distance the* dukha.

A Message from Jenny

Here is a good example of what happens when our inner flame is weak and we're faced with a stressor. Little Mathew threw a darling little piece of fire wood my way and I'll let you read on to find out how well I managed to deal with it.

At 22-years-old, on my journey of recovery from anorexia, I landed my first position within the school system teaching Elementary Phys. Ed at an inner city school in Vancouver. Within a few short months of being there, I was taught a tremendous lesson from a six year old boy. As I stood in the doorway of a classroom and summoned my jovial grade 1's into line, little Mathew came running up to me and gave me a big hug. Not knowing what to say, but eager to maintain my full attention, he yelled out, "Ms. K, you're FAT!"

Every cell in my body jolted to a halt and I froze, my breath stuck in my throat. Even though a part of me knew he was just being a pesky little six-year-old, his words shook like a harsh accusation, which I attached massive negative meaning to. Like a wet log thrown onto an already weak fire, I was so shaken off center that I slid back into a number of light days of eating before reclaiming my sense of balance again.

After noticing the reaction that followed this innocent little boy's statement, a very loud voice inside me sang out "Jenny, you're in big trouble if a six year old boy can throw you off center so dramatically. You clearly lack essential inner qualities to effectively deal with life." At this point I was well on my way to physical recovery but my emotional and mental resilience needed serious work. I was able to see that my self-worth was still inappropriately linked to the beauty of my physical body and the opinions of others, and I intuitively knew there was something deeper I needed to rely on.

The feeling of being that weak and vulnerable to the storms of life still lingers clearly in my memory. I am pleased to say that today this feeling of instability is indeed a memory and not a current reality. That's because I tend my agni, my inner fire every day by throwing dry, fire fueling wood (like compassion and self love) on a strong and healthy flame.

Jenny

Healthy emotions

> Childhood and adolescence are critical windows of opportunity for setting down the essential emotional habits that will govern our lives.[21]

> Deficiencies in emotional intelligence heighten a spectrum of risks, from depression and violence to eating disorders and drug abuse. I can foresee a day when education will routinely include essential human competencies such as self awareness, self-control, empathy, the art of listening, resolving conflict and cooperation.[22]

Emotional literacy is a term that encourages us to become skillful at identifying our emotional landscape from moment to moment, followed by the ability to regulate and balance our emotions. Similarly, emotional intelligence, according to Daniel Goleman, is the ability to rein in emotional impulses, to read another's innermost feelings and to handle relationships smoothly. (Emotional Intelligence, by Daniel Goleman, page xxiii).

Just as we develop skills in reading and writing, it is important that we become aware of our emotions and learn to express them appropriately in order for us to live resiliently, in order to remain within the stream of well-being.

Recent research shows that out of all the human intelligences, emotional and social intelligence are as important, if not more so, in determining one's fulfillment in life.

Researchers have known for years that emotional intelligence contributes to occupational success. At Harvard University, researchers discovered over three decades ago that people who were best at identifying others' emotions were more successful in their work as well as in their social lives.[23]

Despite this knowledge of the importance of emotional intelligence, our emotional life is often frowned upon, or ridiculed today, with statements such as "let's not be so emotional." Yet we all know that every Olympic medal that's ever been won and every health battle that's been overcome occurred because people had emotion, and lots of it, channeled in a certain direction. They used their passion to fuel their belief in themselves and to charge their actions. If you have human emotion, you have one of the most important natural resources at your disposal. But we need to ensure we're using the right ones, and using them in the right way, in order to be resilient and strong like the healthy tree in the forest.

There are many emotions that we can experience in the run of a day, but the sad reality is that most us predominantly experience the ones that make us feel crappy. Our challenge, then, is to discern which emotions contribute to our feeling bad and the situations that bring them about. We must then become practiced at focusing on experiences and emotions that help us feel good.

Neuroscience has determined that our brains have a pliable plastic quality, with the ability to change and morph. Exciting news, isn't it? Rick Hanson has taken that discovery one step further by noting that we tend to lean into negativity, and away from positivity. This draw toward negativity has served us historically by keeping us hyper alert to danger, enabling us to anticipate where the next attack will come from so as to avoid harm. The day you're

---

[21] Daniel Goleman, *Emotional Intelligence, Why It Can Matter More Than IQ*, (Bantam Books, 1997), xxii
[22] Ibid. p. xxiv
[23] Matthew Fox, "Putting Emotional Intelligence to Work" (Paper presented at the Annual Meeting of the Society for Industrial and Organizational Psychology, New Orleans, LA, April 15, 2000)

having today is almost completely different from the day your grandmother, or great grandmother had at your age. While the threats to our wellbeing are almost totally different, our reaction to a stressor is the same. Since we're not threatened in the same way as our foremothers, we are faced with the challenge and opportunity to alter our inner dialogue and therefore reconstruct our brains, so that we have more peaceful, positive life experiences.

Consider the analogy from the great yoga sage, Swami Sivananda, who likened tending to a garden when it comes to meditation and positive thinking. The practices we're learning here help to fine tune our discernment so we can weed out the negative, worrisome thoughts and nurture the positive thoughts into blossoms that help us feel good. And we all know that when we feel good about ourselves, we feel stronger, more confident and more able to weather the storms of life.

> When you take in positive experiences, you are not only growing flowers in your mind. You are growing new neural circuits in your brain. [24]

Pratipaksha Bhavana

According to the yogic tradition, a healthy mind shapes a healthy body. To maintain a healthy mental state requires us to clear our minds of patterns of sadness, despair, worry, stress, tension, anger, hatred, greed and pride. That may sound like a big task, but the following structure is a time-tested way of quieting the darker tendencies of the mind while replacing them with constructive mind states.

The ancient yogi, Patanjali, who understood the tremendous impact that our beliefs have on our well-being, designed a practice called *Pratipaksha Bhavana*. *Pratipaksha Bhavana*, which translates into "moving to the other side of the mansion (our being)," is the method by which we can turn our awareness from a negative, toxic focus in a more positive direction. This ancient practice has been adapted by contemporary therapies to effectively change our states of mind, regulate our emotions and enhance our ability to live within the stream of well being.

Have you ever considered that you have the amazing freedom to choose the thoughts you think? It's true, but our challenge lies in taking charge of that untamed inner roommate who thinks random thoughts all day long.

What we think and feel in this moment is a self-fulfilling prophecy that determines what we become tomorrow. For many of us, our inner dialogue is loaded with worn out negative messages. We all have a story about who we think we are, and too often it is a story that leaves us feeling small, powerless and contracted. We were all born with a story. It is our choice to live out the story we were born with or create one that lights up our life and nurtures our wholeness. With this awareness of how our thoughts and beliefs influence our well-being, we can begin to shift from being victims of circumstance where we live out our lives unconsciously, to becoming architects of our own reality. Within you lies the power to transform any thought pattern, habit or behavior, you just need the tools and support to do it skillfully.

Let's begin by identifying a thought or belief we desire to change, for example, "everyone I grow close to ends up leaving me" or "the world is an unsafe and frightening place to live in." Take a moment to feel the negative effects that these simple statements have on your

---

[24] Rick Hanson, *Hardwiring Happiness*, (Harmony Books, 2013), 9

body, imagine the long term affects these beliefs would have on your life? Now search for a belief of your own that is limiting your enjoyment of life. Are you ready to transform it into a statement that is more life giving? The following steps are considered the 3 As:

ADMIT

The first step in transforming a negative thought pattern is to admit we have a limiting, fire-snuffing belief or an unhealthy emotional pattern that we are ready to change. We admit to ourselves that we've fallen into the dark hole. Before we can rise to a healthier place in our life, we must first become clear on where we stand right now. This may take some courage to be honest about your current life situation, but the alternative is the victim stance which gets you no where fast. A key point at this phase is to identify the issue, without identifying yourself as the issue. You *are not* a procrastinator, or a lazy slug, or an angry grouch, (these are all labels). You *have* a habit of being or doing life in a way that doesn't serve your highest good and now is the perfect time to make a change. Write down the thought, belief or habit you are ready to release.

ALLOW

We allow whatever negative pattern is present to be there, but this time we don't feed it with attention or energy. We acknowledge any judgments we may have about falling, yet again, into the dark hole, and we let them go in order to let the issue go. We recognize the presence of the negative thought and take control of it immediately so its flame doesn't expand in our minds. We don't necessarily need to approach this phase aggressively, (although it is an option), but instead we can deal with more passively by simply withdrawing our attention. For example, we choose to leave the junk food in the cupboard and turn our attention to the basket of fresh fruit. This phase is also called the phase of dilution, where we start to dilute our usual attention to the junk food with thoughts of healthier options. This phase requires the presence of the compassionate witness, the part of you that can watch the ingrained unhealthy habit, without judgment or criticism. Criticizing yourself for having the pattern will only feed the issue with your attention, which is not where you want your focus to be. We not only watch the habitual tendency, but we also notice the excuses that we have conjured up to justify it, such as "I'm a weak person and this habit is more powerful than me" or "my parents are right, I can't do anything successfully." Don't argue with your habit, just remove your attention. It is helpful to emphasize the act of stopping the thought pattern in its tracks. Below are some fun options to help you do that:
- Speak out loud "change," "stop!" or "back off"
- You could write your intention, such as 'peace' or 'freedom' on a thick elastic band and wear it around your wrist. When you are triggered or tempted to engage the habit you are changing, gently snap the elastic band on your wrist and recite the word written on it.
- You can keep a crystal, or a stone from your favourite beach in your pocket and rub it as you speak your mantra.

- Place your hands into *apana mudra* - join the thumb with the middle and ring finger to flush negativity from your system.
- Take a warrior stance, or pull up the image of a stance of power in your mind if you're not free to strike a pose in the moment.
- Stop what you are doing, remove yourself and take three deep breaths, blowing out the negative thought. Follow your momentary cleanse with the image of golden light pouring in through your crown, filling you with light.
- Shake it off by shaking your limbs or play some funky tunes and dance.
- Rest your hands on your heart, give yourself a hug, or rub your forehead as a self soothing technique.

Act

As we remove our attention from the negative pattern, we choose to **act** in a way that aligns with our highest values and intentions. At this point you can repeat a fire-fueling statement that you've created with passion and belief until the negative, limiting, fire-snuffing mechanism is transformed into a fire-fueling habit that enhances your life. But choosing an alternative, opposite or more positive focus for your mind can be difficult as negative patterns may be very familiar. You are encouraged to draw from the strength of others by thinking of a person who is successful, healthy or peaceful. Relax your facial expression and try smiling softly, filling your heart with compassion.

By acting positively, we let goodness in and choose to live within the stream of wellbeing. We choose to walk around the dark hole and eventually avoid falling into the abyss by taking a different route altogether. Over time, by turning up the volume on the healthy feelings and turning down the unhealthy habit, the positive completely replaces the negative. Your negative pattern may return again and again, but with disciplined effort it will diminish in power as your flame grows brighter. One day, you will notice that the negative pattern has disappeared from your life and you are living with new levels of joy and possibility. This is the process of *Pratipaksha Bhavana*.

The 3A's help us to accelerate change in our lives by reflecting on our behavior patterns and then intentionally taking alternative action that will create different results. As a Girl on Fire, you can choose to take charge of your life and your actions, once you realize that every choice you make influences the health of your body, your mind and your emotions.

As we begin to understand the immensity of our natural inner strength, we realize that we can indeed overcome all negativity and any unhealthy pattern in our lives. There is boundless light within you and all you need to do is open the door on darkness. Just a crack will let the light seep in, eventually banishing the darkness. Negativity is like a mirage-- it's not the most real, authentic part of who you are. The real you is sparkling with radiant light.

The greatest attainment in life is not material wealth, academic achievement or career success, but the transformation of one's personality. That is what provides us with lasting peace and enjoyment.

Individual reflection

Take five minutes for silent reflection on how your life might change and open up with the removal of just one limiting belief. Our work here is to get crystal clear about how we want to feel each day and then be intentional about choosing thoughts that support that feeling, which then informs our beliefs and determines the shape of our lives.

Record the answers that came to your mind about how you want to feel in your life.

ANXIETY

Let's spend some time examining two of the most common, (and devastating) factors that threaten our mental and physical resilience today: anxiety and stress.

Recommendations from the ancient Ayurvedic sages

With regards to Ayurveda, anxiety is a vata or air-imbalanced condition that is growing rapidly amongst teens. It might be helpful to breeze through the vata pacifying recommendations, which also serve in calming anxiety. Note that even if you aren't a vata type, it is the most unstable dosha and the first one to slide off-kilter so we all need to nurture our vata tendencies. Also remember that vata is most unstable in the fall so be mindful about staying warm and well nourished, with warm soups and hot drinks. A hat will help to contain heat in your body as well. Overtaxing yourself with school work, extracurricular activities or excessive screen time can set vata imbalance in motion so you may need to back off to find a healthy work/rest balance. Establishing a regular, manageable schedule is essential for vata happiness so keep your daily routine as consistent as possible.

Anxiety is something that can affect all of us, but it's especially common during adolescence because there are so many changes occurring within your body, mind and emotions. Remember, you are in the first major transition in your life, which can test your ability to cope effectively with life's challenges.

The trouble with anxiety is that it robs us of the fun in life and inhibits our ability to participate in our lives. And if we're not showing up fully in life, we're not sharing our light. That's a problem because the world needs what you and only you can offer!

Although anxiety can feel totally overwhelming, there are many ways to deal with it, a few of which we'll explore here. The key to healing anxiety is to face it and address it, since in most cases anxiety doesn't just disappear on its own.

Let's examine anxiety to get to know it a bit better, as discussed in "The Anxiety Workbook for Teens" by Lisa M Schab.

- Think of a time in your recent past when you experienced anxiety. What does anxiety feel like inside? Here are some words that may help to describe it: uneasiness, apprehension, uncertainty, worry, fear, nervousness, a melt down, freaking out, panic, stress.
- If you were to rate your anxiety on a scale of 1-10, one being none at all and 10 being a full-blown panic attack, how intense is your anxiety most days?

- Take a few deep breaths and notice where anxiety tends to arise in your body? What thoughts do you think when you're gripped by anxiety? Are there other emotions present as well, like fear, anger or loneliness? Draw a stick figure in the space below and draw, shade or write your anxiety symptoms in the area(s) you feel it.
- Since our emotional health can be inherited from our family, do you suppose you learned anxiety from someone in your life? (no blame is necessary, we're just seeking to understand).
- How do you currently deal with anxiety when it pays you a visit?
- What happens to your inner flame and your passion for life when anxiety consumes you?

Did you know that changing the way we look at life and shifting our perspective (as we are learning to do) can change the way we react to stress and help with anxiety?

STRESS

Did you know that stress is the number one killer in the Western world?

Stress can be described as strain, pressure or tension resulting from a specific demand. Sometimes stress can serve us well, in healthy doses. For example, when weight bearing exercise stresses, and consequently strengthens, bone tissue. Or when we're called to step out of our comfort zone to do something new, and in so doing we acquire new skills. While examples of healthy stress aren't too hard to find, examples of unhealthy stress inundate our lives in unprecedented ways.

There are three different kinds of stress that most people face:
- Physical: the kind of stress that directly affects the body, like too much or too little activity or work, or poor diet choices.
- Chemical stress: the kind of stress brought on from an overload of toxic influences, such as smoke, alcohol, prescription drugs or pollution.
- Emotional stress: the kind of stress that's created from emotional turmoil, like disharmony within our intimate relationships.

Stress can range from a mildly irritating experience such as a misunderstanding with a friend, or being late for an appointment to a major life crisis, like a family illness or a final exam. Regardless of the intensity, the effects of stress over time add up, and most of us live day to day without an outlet, like we once had.

Just 100 years ago we spent 90% of our time outdoors, amongst the healing elements of nature, connected to the rhythms of life. Today, we spend 90% of our waking hours indoors, watching TV or using other technology and breathing stagnant air.

Did you know that up to 70% of people spend six or more hours a day sitting?

Going back even further than 100 years ago, in ancient times, humans lived very different lives from how we live today and they faced very different challenges. The human body is miraculously designed to react instantaneously to a stressor with a spike in hormones that signals us to act fast, with our survival on the line. When the prehistoric human was faced with a sudden encounter with a wild beast, the brain would tell the body that a threat was present and then with the help of hormones such as adrenaline, the body would then react at lightning speed, either fleeing by running away or staying to fight it out. Either option required physical exertion, which would disperse the stress hormones, enabling the body's systems to return to normal when the threat was either scared off or killed.

Today, even though our stressors are very different (for example, a wild beast versus cyber bullying), our bodies still react the same way and release the same stress hormones. And while our stressful scenarios have changed, these hormones still cause the body to prepare for action by increasing our heart rate, quickening our breath and putting our nervous system on red alert. Where the big problem lies today is in the absence of that energetic outlet. Stress hormones get trapped in our body's system, leading to a lingering state of anxiety and restlessness.

Stress tends to show up in our bodies as muscular tension, digestive irregularities, bowel issues, low sexual energy, compromised immunity and insomnia. In the presence of stress, the heart rate speeds up, our breathing becomes shallow and our nostrils flair, as we prepare to fight or flee. The blood abandons digestion and goes to our muscles to support this possibility of fleeing. The blood also starts to clot in preparation for injury, even though most of our stressors are long term and don't immediately involve bodily harm. The body's reaction to the creation of blood clots is what causes cardiovascular (heart) disease. Who knew there is so much going on during a stressful event!

The mental and emotional reactions to chronic stress appear as anger, worry, fear, insecurity, obsessive compulsive behavior, moodiness, indecision, depression, impatience and seriousness. It's not hard to see how living in this state for long periods of time rob us of energy, eventually leading to disease.

Have you noticed any of these symptoms appearing in your life or in the lives of your loved ones?

The following are a number of stress related conditions that can arise after prolonged exposure to stress:
- Adrenal fatigue, low energy
- Chronic fatigue
- Thyroid problems
- Headaches
- Environmental illness
- Blood-sugar problems
- Food allergies
- Poor concentration
- Easily overwhelmed, nervous
- Dizziness upon standing
- Anxiety disorder
- Clinical depression
- Bad temper
- Shortness of breath
- Circulation issues, cold extremities
- Muscle soreness
- Sugar and caffeine cravings
- Recurrent colds or infections
- Digestive issues

- Weight gain or loss
- High or low blood pressure

How many of these signs apply to you? If over half of these symptoms sound familiar, you likely have a stress related issue which is taxing your system, challenging your body's ability to maintain long-term, vibrant health.

Simply put, chronic, unmanaged stress causes death. So much so that, 89% of all visits to the doctor are for stress-related symptoms. With the sad reality that more heart attacks occur on Monday mornings than any other time of the week, we can see the importance of emotional well-being and career fulfillment in our lives.

So trying times call for trying a new approach.

We can learn to skillfully deal with the small, yet significant stressors by applying the tools we've learned in previous lessons each and every day. We can also learn to regulate our emotional state by strengthening the reasoning part of our brain and calming the emotionally reactive region of the brain, which tends to imagine the worst.

The next time you're faced with a stressful situation, here are a few stress management suggestions that will strengthen your overall resilience:

- **Think big picture**—instead becoming narrow focused, making a small stressor a really big deal, expand your perspective and ask yourself "What's the long-term impact of this setback?"
- **Stay present**— stress is rarely solely about the event in the moment. Much of our stress comes from the memory of a past stressor and the fear that our future will involve more of what we've already endured. When we draw our minds into the present moment, we can see the situation more clearly and calmly for what it is. We can use the 1:2 ratio breathing, letting the exhale release tension as it activates the rest and digest part of our nervous system and slows our heart rate down.
- **Practice compassion**—if someone's causing you distress, imagine what challenges they might be facing in their lives. When we shift our awareness from our own struggles and consider the other person's life situation, it's much easier to understand their side, which helps us to calm down as well.
- **Healing sounds**—activate your brain's reward system by speaking calmly and using words that soothe your inner turmoil like "I'm relaxing now" or "Everything's just fine." Exhaling to sounds like shhhh and haaa have comforting reactions within, starting with a higher pitch, slowly lowering as you breathe out.
- **"Naming What Is" exercise**—labeling our emotion in the moment helps to reduce the activation of the reactive part of the brain and engages the reasoning part of the brain (see Omwork).
- **Learn optimism**—when something doesn't go as planned expect to be delighted with support and positive surprises. Optimism buffers the effects of stress and helps us become more resilient, leading to bounce-back moments. This takes practice because it's not a natural instinct for most of us, but try visualizing the best-case scenario for a current challenge and imagine that this is all part of the greater plan to help propel you toward the highest vision you hold for your life.
- **Movement:** remember the benefits of yoga. It's the perfect solution for optimizing our health, resiliency and joy. And virtually everyone can do it! Even a short movement practice draws us back into the stream of well-being by:

- - Strengthening muscle
  - Improving our posture
  - Increasing our flexibility
  - Balancing our weight
  - Calming our mind
  - Improving our self-esteem
  - Fostering spiritual connection
- **Soothe your senses:** play soft music, curl up in a cozy blanket, soak in the elements of nature, drink a warm cup of calming tea, etc. What do your senses appreciate when stress arises in your life?

Omwork

Dress rehearsal: take some time on your own to journal about a recent experience that ignited negativity within you. If you can't think of one right now, create a scenario in your mind that might trigger a negative pattern that you're keen to transform. By identifying this scenario you've already done the first A: you've admitted you have a trigger. Next just notice the toxic emotions that arise when you think about the situation. Finally, and most importantly, write down as many positive ways you could act that would create sukha and ease, instead of the downer feelings of dukha. Let yourself have fun with this last step, and even ask your mentor what suggestions she might have to add to the list. You may want to circle or highlight the answers that resonate best with you, and continue in your spare time to imagine yourself acting in these ways the next time the trigger strikes.

Example

Every time Sally's parents argued (which was a lot), she would instantly feel guilty, like it was her fault they didn't get along. Her coping mechanism (and dukha creating action) was to tuck herself into the bathroom and cut herself. While she knew this was unkind and dangerous, it seemed to ease the pain and release the negativity that boiled up inside. After learning the 3A's, the next time the arguing began, she had the list of positive actions at the ready on her phone. This time, she removed herself from the toxic fighting, sat down and took a few grounding BREATHs, admitting she was in her trigger state. She was able to notice the negativity arise and spoke out loud to herself, "I'm feeling sad, lonely, guilty and angry." She took a few more exhalations, letting herself sigh with a vocal haaaa and asked herself what positive action she wanted to take to soak in the sukha. In that moment, she chose to play her favorite song that reminded her of her inner treasures of self-worth and confidence. Before long, the moment passed and so did her impulse to self-harm.

Lights action, real life practice: the next time a storm strikes your life, large or small, stand firm, and practice BREATH process and tune your awareness into your inner flame. If you have the time in the moment, go through the three A's, admit you've been triggered, allow the feeling to be there by **<u>naming what is</u>** (be careful not to feed this energy though), and then **choose** to act in a way that supports your greatness.

If the issue is still lingering in your mind, instead of letting it roam through your mind untamed for hours, you can give yourself a timed period of about 2-5 minutes to completely indulge the issue by ruminating, ranting, writing, whatever you wish. Once you've given it a contained amount of airtime, stop your rumination and turn your mind to a solution. Take a few cleansing breaths and go in search of beauty.

Seek counsel from your mentor, asking her about a time in her life when she was challenged deeply. What tools did she use? How did they work? What did she learn?

Research and read about famous people who have overcome adversity, and let yourself absorb their strength and wisdom.

Make a list of other ideas for cleansing negativity or dukha to make space for sukha.

Affirmations

Every day I commit to soaking in the sukha (ease) and distancing the dukha (negativity).

By practicing Admit, Allow and Act, I am becoming more resilient to life's obstacles.

With each breath I take, I release stress and relax.

Understanding that stress doesn't serve me, I steadfastly commit to living with peace.

Personal additions:

Physical Posture

Gathering and Grounding Flow

Mindful Movement Class - Week 6

NOTE: This is the Mindful Movement Class to accompany Week 6. For consistency and ease, we recommend the video series of these classes available at www.GirlOnFire.ca.

Weekly theme – Resilience
Mountain Pose with Fall Out Breaths Neck Stretches Arm Vinyasa Kidney flow Wide legged forward bend with scalp massage Full body flow Embracing the Tree pose Balancing Tree pose Classical Namaskara, with Crescent Lunge The Crane flapping its wings **Feature Posture:** Gather and Ground Flow Locust with fingers interlocked behind back Saddle pose — single leg Upward dog Table Top with undulating spine Cow Face Pose **Partner Posture:** Seated Wide Angle Forward Bend Sukhasana with Centering Flow Savasana/Relaxation Pose
Girl on Fire closing To acknowledge the three centers of Power, Love and Insight: Rise to sitting and bring palms together. Lift hands so that thumbs touch the mid eye point and say: "Guided by insight" Now draw hands to heart, one palm on heart center in the middle of the chest and the other palm resting on top of the first hand and say: "I listen to my heart's desire" Now take the top hand and slide it down so it rests on the navel, with the first hand remaining on the heart and say: "And take positive, powerful action in the world"

Notes

Week 7 – Discipline

This week's focus is to gain deeper understanding of:
- Developing Discipline
- Technology and Social Media
- Healthy technology management
- The healing power of touch

For many of us, when we hear the word discipline, we think of an external force ensuring we obediently follow rules and, as needed, inflicting punishment. But in this program, discipline is referred to as a practice of inward training with the intention to personally grow, develop our skills and become more effective in our lives. And with the abundance of influences vying for our attention, never before in the history of humanity have we needed inner discipline more than we do today. It takes discipline to stay within the stream of well-being, and just like a mother is to her child, we must become skilled at saying no to our senses.

A Message from Jenny

I have always been a very disciplined and self-motivated kind of person, which has mostly served me well, except the time when my discipline, (what the ancient yogis called drishti or mental focus) became misdirected.

The summer before university, about four months into my anorexic frenzy, I thought it was a good idea to prepare for my swimming lab that fall by doing a few laps of our lake. In the past it was common for me to throw the canoe over my shoulders and head down for a solo paddle when the water was calm. As strong and capable as I had always been, I was not at all used to depending on anyone for physical support. So when mom demanded that she accompany me by paddling beside me, I was furious but relented.

My body was different now and mom knew it. Although I was dangerously thin and visibly ill, just four months prior I was a healthy capable girl and part of me still perceived myself that way. It only took a few gulps of water for me to realize that I was indeed living in a different body. Despite my diminishing physical strength, I was motivated by my weight loss. I was skinny and proud of it, and viewed it as a great achievement. My self-discipline had become misdirected under the influence of diseased thinking.

The next summer, after a full year of university, I returned home to work as a day camp leader. One sunny afternoon, in the comforts of my home, I thought I'd push my edge and try some yogurt with raisins. As I poured the yogurt into the little bowl I had chosen, I could feel the heat rising from the pit of my belly and a quake of panic surged through my system. As the anxiety rose to a point of unbearable intensity, I threw the bowl into the sink and took off running. I didn't know or care where I was going, I just needed to get away from the feeling that burned through my body, consuming me like a cancer. As I approached the far end of our beach, my outdoor sanctuary, I realized that I was running from the agony of feeling entirely out of control in my life.

Just as I was collapsing with exhaustion, my mother who had quietly followed, caught me in her arms. In that moment, huddled together on the beach, I acknowledged that I had lost my way and couldn't turn the page on this situation now, even if I wanted to. This was my first realization that my whole being had been hijacked by a dark and deadly force, and I was afraid. "It's gonna be okay Jenny dear, it's gonna be okay." I clung to mother's words as she rocked me like she'd done so many years ago.

What started off as a grand achievement in self-discipline had somehow turned into a death trap. This was my trophy for attaining the skinny images that the media encouraged? I began to question whether skinny was worth the cost.

Over time, I came to the conclusion that I was indeed going to die if I didn't change the course of my life, pronto. I finally realized that no one else could do this for me, it was my mess and only I could clean it up. Ironically, I also knew that the exact inner quality of focused discipline that got me into this addicted state was the same quality I would need, in hefty supply, to get me out.

Each day I woke up and directed my discipline toward my new focus of reclaiming my life. Day after day, little by little, through disciplined effort, my life began to transform. Had I decided to change the course of my life years earlier when the patterning wasn't so deeply ingrained, it likely would have required less effort. But turning a corner in a peppy 16 foot motor boat takes a different skill set than turning a thousand foot cruise ship. One turns on a dime instantly and efficiently, while the other requires strategy, space, patience and of course discipline.

Jenny

Developing Discipline

Achieving anything in life requires disciplined effort. In mindfulness practice, we are challenged to come to the cushion, or the yoga mat and do the same thing each day but with fresh awareness and curiosity about the moment, which is always changing. Sometimes discipline is required to do the same thing every day, if it's a health promoting practice such as meditation, or movement, or drinking water, or taking supplements. Other times, discipline is required to make a change, as in the case of changing an unhealthy pattern.

Tony Robbins claims there are two pains that everyone has to live with: the pain of regret or the pain of discipline. Many people end up with the pain of regret because they didn't take the time to ask themselves what they want their life to be about. They just blindly live out their life without a plan, without listening to their heart. You are being given the opportunity to reflect on how you want to live your life, but the answer to this question is but one piece of the puzzle. The other piece is the discipline required to move you in that direction.

Take a moment to practice the BREATH process, and in your minds eye, name what is present for you right now. Allow a picture of your life right now to form. Now let your imagination take you 365 days from today, when you'll be one year older. What are you doing and who are you doing it with? Are you happy? Are you fulfilled? Are you struggling with an issue you are faced with today? Has it changed at all? Can you see how important discipline is as a key element to creating the life you want?

Time will go on, your life will continue to unfold, and how you choose to live it is totally up to you. Without discipline, we are all destined to the pain of regret. But with focus and the right supports in place, we can experience the pain of discipline, which can be painful indeed, but on the other side of hard work is the life of your dreams.

A healthy, happy, and fulfilling life is available to all of us, but some of us will succumb to small thinking, or excuses, or sleep walking through life. It's those of us who choose the path of self-discipline who will reap the rewards of focused effort.

There is a wonderful story in a yogic text about a great warrior named Arjuna. (Pardon the male references but all yogis were men back in the day, haven't things changed today?) Arjuna was known by his tribesmen as the best archer around. One day, his teacher instructed his class to look at the bird in the tree before them. He then asked each one individually what they saw when he looked at the bird. One student said he saw the claws of the bird gripping the branch, while another saw the bird's beautiful tail. When the teacher asked Arjuna what he saw, he said with an unwavering gaze, that all he saw was the eye of the bird. Arjuna was the best archer because he was so intently focused on the target.

In today's world, it is very difficult for us to practice focused attention with the many distractions in our immediate environment. In fact, our attention has become so fragmented that video and TV clips are a mere one second long. We've got YouTube, Google, social media, online shopping, etc. etc. all vying for our attention. The field of media and marketing has become an advanced study in psychology, refining how they present products in the exact way that will capture your desire.

Desire is the way of the senses, and your senses will always want to be fed and yet they will never be satisfied. In yoga, there are two different ways of living; living in a way that is captive to your senses, where you spend your whole life searching for sensory satisfaction in everything you do. The act of searching is filled with the energy of striving and craving, both of which drain our energy stores. When you do finally satisfy your senses, you're often feeding your body and mind things that cause ill health.

The other way of living is living in accordance with what we know to be healthy and best for a long and happy life. This requires that we constrain our senses, perhaps drinking water instead of pop, or sleeping without our phone. The more we do this, the more we turn away from unhealthy habits and focus more on healthy habits, a very interesting thing occurs; we start to crave healthy things and no longer feel slave to our senses. This may take time but it's worth it, and you're worth it!

Can you see how essential it is that you develop discipline in order to focus on your own target and pursue your own dreams? Otherwise, if we're not careful, a year will go by and we'll have nothing to show for it but 10, 000 meaningless text messages. So many people leave this earth without fulfilling their calling, what they came here to do. We are all meant for greatness in some way and discipline is the vehicle that's driving us to the victory party. And the exciting thing about life is that we're all invited!

Desire for anything lives in the heart, and deep inner desire to fulfill our dreams is something to pay attention to. Great ideas come from the mind. When we have authentic desire to pursue a great idea, we need to access the power of discipline. Discipline and the energy required to take effective action comes from our core, our center of power. Our movement practices are designed to help you build strength in your center of power.

Technology and Social Media

Modern technology has enhanced our lives by providing us with resources we otherwise would never have exposure to. Social media helps us feel connected to the global human community, fostering tolerance for racial differences and a whole new sense of connectedness with people across the world. We can do it all on social media, from intimate contact to a global conversation. There is amazing potential for connection, activism and even employment through this worldwide communication system, without even leaving our homes.

Through this instant and vast connection power, social media can support us on our journey to positively evolve and personally develop.

But it also has major hazards as well. It can dull our intellectual fire by consuming our attention to the point of exhaustion and diminish our communication to simplistic one liners, which can lead to superficial dialogue and severe relationship limitations. It also allows people to lash out negatively and aggressively, in ways they might never do so in person, because they have the distance to buffer their assault without seeing the direct impact of their words. It's easy to find yourself in a group chat and suddenly realize you're engaging in gossip, or spreading rumors through toxic conversations.

Our mindfulness practices can come in handy at this point, providing us with the self awareness to step away from the conversation, take a few deep breaths and ask ourselves if the quality of conversation aligns with our intention to make positive ripples in the world.

Humans need regular doses of heart connections and using technology for this purpose can contribute to our overall sense of happiness. However, personal contact has a greater impact on our well being than impersonal, or distant contact. So whenever possible, use Facetime or Skype to bridge the distance. Healthy, human communication is two-sided and requires connection between two or more people. Be sure to remember that the recipient of your texts needs attention as well so practice using "I" a little less and inquire about the other person's well-being. Be curious about their day and ask them questions about life challenges, beyond your own.

In terms of the constant, superficial contact that we can become addicted to, ask yourself if what you are about to send is worthy of consuming your time and theirs. We spend way too much of our lives sending messages that could be shared later in a more meaningful, one-on-one conversation or depending on the importance, not shared at all. Constantly sharing your random, insignificant thoughts not only annoys the recipient but may also cause them to take space from you.

A Girl on Fire uses social media as a means for spreading good will, not ill will, and positively empowering our friends.

Personal growth is something you will work on for the rest of your life. It is an ongoing lifelong project that will bring rewards every day. This is the process of becoming a Girl on Fire. The inner treasures we are learning about in this program can be cultivated and strengthened with the use of technology, but you must also apply discipline to stay focused on your deepest desires, instead of succumbing to lower, more negative and even violent influences that are so readily available.

BE YOUR OWN VIGILANTE

Images, stories and communication all stay in our subconscious mind and either contribute positively or negatively to our lives. Negativity and violence diminish our inner flame and can weaken our sense of confidence and faith in the world. Within a few minutes of channel surfing the TV, you'll likely see scenario's of sexual exploitation, objectification of the female body and violence against women. Be careful with the content you expose yourself to, remembering that it may stay with you for years to come.

Read through the list of inner treasures and choose one or two that you want to build on. Now use technology in your favor by seeking out groups, websites and information on the subject. By focusing your attention on whatever it is you wish to develop, it is like you are strength training the fibers of that treasure.
1) Self awareness
2) Self Worth
3) Confidence
4) Discernment
5) Resilience
6) Discipline
7) Optimism
8) Contentment
9) Connection
10) Essence

Social media is a very powerful aid in our well-being. As a Girl on Fire, we know that when we do personal work to clear out the fire-snuffing factors in our lives, whether it's negative inner dialogue or exposure to violent influences, we make room for the healthy, joyful and beautiful aspects of life. And when our inner flame is aglow with beauty and inspiration, all of the people in our lives are uplifted too; our family members, our friends, our communities and the entire planet. Remember that your highest purpose is to enhance and improve humanity. The next time you're searching the internet, watching YouTube or chatting online, ask yourself if your actions are in-line with your intentions to be an example of well-being and inspiration.

BOUNDARIES AND SOCIAL MEDIA

Our modern technological age, with its ability to send information around the world within seconds, requires us to be very careful about what content we share with anyone. No matter who you are communicating with, the moment you press send you have no control about where that information will go and who will see it. It is essential that you practice self-awareness in the few moments before you send anything and ask yourself, "Am I okay with this information or photo being shared with the world?" That's the possibility for everything you share.

There's less tolerance for the boring bits in life. Part of my fieldwork is to stand at stop signs and watch what happens in cars. The moment people stop, they reach for their phones. They can't be alone with their thoughts. Parents need to show kids that there's no need to panic if you're without your phone. If you don't teach children its okay to be alone, they will only know how to be lonely.

Have you noticed yourself or others filling even a few second break with screen time? Ever notice what happens to your breathing when you search your text messages?[25]

What we know

- 92% of teens report going online daily — including 24% who say they go online "almost constantly,"[26]
- Some 88% of teens have or have access to cell phones or smartphones and 90% of those teens with phones exchange texts. A typical teen sends and receives 30 texts per day[27]
- The average phone user spends 3.6 hours of their day on their device and the more you use your phone, the more severe your addiction gets. The researchers also found that those who scored highest for narcissism were the most likely candidates for being addicted to their phones.[28]
- A study by the University of Chicago Booth School of Business shows that the desire to check a social network like Twitter or Facebook is stronger than the need to smoke a cigarette or drink alcohol.[29]

The healing power of touch

As Turkle says in her book title, we are a culture who expects more from technology and less from each other, and that's dangerous because we are becoming more and more disconnected from one another and yet we still crave and even require the goodness that comes from true human connection.

Relationships are an undeniable reality of human existence and many people have lost the essential interpersonal skills to sustain healthy connections. Once upon a time the only option we had for relating with one another was face to face contact. Today, with 90% of people owning cell phones and the multiple modes of communication available, the frequency of person to person interactions have diminished significantly, and with that, our sense of belonging and connected. And while our communication has become leaps and bounds more efficient, no screen device can fully replace our basic need for physical human contact.

---

[25] Sherry Turkle, Alone, Together: Why we expect more from technology and less from each other, Real Simple magazine, accessed September 2016
http://www.realsimple.com/work-life/technology/social-media-psychology
[26] "Teens, Social Media & Technology Overview 2015", Pew Research Center, accessed September 2016, http://www.pewinternet.org/2015/04/09/teens-social-media-technology-2015/
[27] Ibid
[28] "Smartphone addiction Statistics reveal 1 in 8 are addicted to their phones" iDigital Times, March 2015, http://www.idigitaltimes.com/smartphone-addiction-statistics-reveal-1-8-are-addicted-their-phones-419714
[29] "Study: Is Facebook more addictive than alcohol or cigarettes?", Digital Trends, accessed September 2016, http://www.digitaltrends.com/social-media/study-is-facebook-more-addictive-than-alcohol-or-cigarettes/

In today's North American world, with so much confusion around physical touch, we've made the dire mistake of prohibiting any human contact. We live with so many warnings and rules around touch (mostly for good reason) that we've lost contact with one another altogether. The term skin hunger is a very real issue today, as physical human contact is considered one of the top four needs, on the heels of food, water, and rest.

Have you heard of Juan Mann? He's the founder of the free hugs movement. In the midst of personal difficulties, he attended a party where a person approached him and gave him a spontaneous hug. He instantly felt better. Realizing he was deprived of meaningful human contact, he began offering free hugs to perfect strangers, as random acts of kindness—and it worked!

If we could open our hearts and live more affectionately, our lives might transform in the presence of a little human contact.

The necessity of human touch:
- Touch is one of the necessary factors in proper growth and development, as studies show that babies in orphanages who were raised without it, often died.
- Touch is essential for the healthy development of emotional and social intelligence, and our ability to relate to people around us.
- Touch contributes to the deep bonds between parents and children, establishing healthy, lifelong attachments.
- Touch boosts our immunity, enabling us to fight off incoming illnesses, viruses and bacteria
- Touch releases oxytocin, known as the bliss hormone, giving us a feeling of love, connection, and comfort, while calming anxiety and agitation in the belly.
- Touch enhances our sense of self worth, which influences our ability to choose healthy, intimate partners.

What are some ways we as humans use artificial ways of satisfy our touch needs?
- Drugs (cocaine is known to produce the same feeling as touch)
- Virtual connection through texting and social media; we do not benefit from having thousands of 'friends' on Facebook. Respectful, loving human contact is a person to person exchange.
- Alcohol, which dissolves our social boundaries, allowing us to reach out without self-consciousness or fear, but often leaving us in a pool of regret and shame the next day.

What are some healthy structures you could incorporate into your own life to satisfy your touch needs?
- Firstly, establish clear boundaries before seeking contact. This is non-sexual, respectful human touch.
- Ask for hugs from friends and family, holding them long enough to count to roughly 30 seconds

- Receive massage therapy
- We are multi-generational beings and connecting to the full spectrum of humanity is important for all of us. You could baby sit little ones, volunteer at the hospital to hold premature babies or visit the elderly
- Doing daily self-massage (abhyanga) with soothing oils is a beautiful way of honoring yourself and satisfying your touch needs.
- There is a saying by respected family therapist, Virginia Satir: "We need four hugs a day for survival. We need eight hugs a day for maintenance. We need twelve hugs a day for growth."

When we feel alone or depressed we naturally withdraw from human interaction, which only worsens the situation. With your new awareness of the importance of touch, you can reach out to a trusted friend, family member or counselor and extend the invitation for a healthy exchange of physical contact.

Omwork

Take the opportunity to incorporate the following tips for healthy technology management into your daily life and journal your experience. At the end of the week do you notice a difference in how you use technology and communicate with your friends?

Set time limits for browsing online. Technology is designed to hold you hostage and keep your attention drawn to the screen.

How much time per day do you believe is reasonable and healthy?

Establish rules like no social media during meals or social time, when commuting and when you're in the bathroom or in bed.

Buy an alarm clock so you don't have to use the phone first thing in the morning. Better yet, consider leaving it outside your bedroom for an uninterrupted sleep and train your body to rise naturally after a full night's sleep.

Be purposeful! If you log in to technology out of boredom with no clear intent, you're more likely to lift your head hours later and wonder where the time went. Be specific in your search and then shut 'er down and call a friend.

Take a weekend off. Taking a full weekend off won't break an addictive habit but it will give you some reprieve from the drive to check status updates every minute.

Affirmations

What I think and feel in this moment is a self-fulfilling prophecy that determines what I become tomorrow.

My life will unfold, whether I make a plan or not, so today I move with discipline in the direction of my dreams.

Through disciplined effort, I limit my exposure to technology and spend time enjoying real life.

By developing healthy relationships, I am fostering self-worth, intimacy and happiness.

Personal additions:

Physical posture

Embracing the Tree, 2-5 minutes

Mindful Movement Class - Week 7

NOTE: This is the Mindful Movement Class to accompany Week 7. For consistency and ease, we recommend the video series of these classes available at www.GirlOnFire.ca.

Weekly theme – Discipline
Note - Yin yoga is a slow, methodical practice, very different from other styles of yoga. According to ancient Chinese Medicine, yin is defined as the shaded side of the slope, associated with qualities such as cold, rest, passivity, tranquility, darkness and introversion. Yang on the other hand, is described as the sunny side of the slope, implying qualities such as heat, stimulation, excitement, action, light and extroversion. Just as each full day contains within it both night (earth/yin) and day (sky/yang), so too do our bodies require time for rest as well as activity. But today, with 24hr services available and the many temptations vying for our attention, it is easy for us to slide outside of our natural rhythms, eating meals and watching shows late into the night or spending excessive amounts of time on technological devices. As a result, most people in the western world live an imbalanced, highly active yang life, which is the energy of fire and output, while the need for inward nourishment that the water element provides is neglected. Our systems (especially our feminine monthly rhythms) require stillness and rest in order function within the stream of wellbeing. This class will provide you with some much-needed time for inner quietude and reflection to help you reconnect with your innate state of harmony, health and balance. Sometimes slowing down to smell the flowers and unplugging to appreciate the moment requires tremendous discipline in our fast paced, overschedule lifestyle, but the rewards are long lasting. Seiza/Hero Pose Earth Salutation from knees Table Pose with forearm stretches Child's Pose Puppy Pose to melted heart pose Downward Dog Dangling/Rag Doll Pose **Featured Posture:** Embracing the Tree Pigeon Pose with quad release Folded Wings Pose Sphinx Pose to Seal Pose Child's Pose **Partner Posture:** Butterfly Pose Seated Forward Fold Supported Bridge Pose Savasana/Pentacle/Relaxation Pose

> **Girl on Fire closing**
>
> To acknowledge the three centers of Power, Love and Insight:
>
> Rise to sitting and bring palms together. Lift hands so that thumbs touch the mid eye point and say: *"Guided by insight"*
>
> Now draw hands to heart, one palm on heart center in the middle of the chest and the other palm resting on top of the first hand and say: *"I listen to my heart's desire"*
>
> Now take the top hand and slide it down so it rests on the navel, with the first hand remaining on the heart and say: *"And take positive, powerful action in the world"*

Notes

Week 8 – Optimism

This week's focus is to gain deeper understanding of:
- Depression
- Why Optimism
- Low and High power posture
- The power of a smile

A Message from Jenny

My grandfather's family lived a simple life as farmers in the remote hills of Kingston Peninsula, New Brunswick. He grew up working hard for every meal, without the convenient amenities we have today. When little Harold was four years old, his mother announced he was going to be a big brother. At the age of five, Harold's whole life changed dramatically. His mother went into labor, at home, as it was done back in the day, and encountered complications—serious ones. After many hours of struggle, just before the doctor arrived, Harold's mother and his new baby brother died.

You can imagine in the early 1900s how sparse the support was for a traumatic event such as this. Harold's Dad, having no tools to effectively deal with the loss of his wife and his new child, dropped into an abyss of depression that stole his joy for the rest of his life. Little Harold, therefore, grew up with his dad, believing that depression was a normal state of being. He spent his childhood working hard in the fields and taking care of his debilitated father, eventually growing up to marry and have two children of his own, one being my Dad, John.

One thing we know for sure about being human is that death is inevitable, in fact, it's a 100% guarantee for everyone alive. And grief is a natural and healthy response to any loss. Unfortunately, many people don't give themselves time to process the loss of a loved one and the energy of grief becomes embedded in their systems. In my dad's case, he came from a line of strong, stoic men, who withheld emotion and the energetic pattern of depression was passed along. With a family history of depression along with his own traumatic life events, John walked through his own darkened path of hopelessness. Interestingly, Clarisa Pinkola Estes says that the opposite of depression is not happiness—it's self-expression.

As for me, because I too grew up with limited resources for dealing with mental illness, I spent much of my life resenting it and fearing it. I think that my anorexia was an attempt to remove myself from life, fearing that adulthood equaled a life of despair as was demonstrated to me as a child. Over the years, as you can see, I've done some deep excavation work into my dysfunctional behavioral patterns, which go back many generations. Through this work of putting the proverbial stick in the spokes, coupled with ancient healing practices, I've not only gained greater understanding of depression, but also deep compassion for it.

I can now see how my father's depression was one of the greatest gifts in my life. **Witnessing him struggle and withdraw from intimate connections during my youth has led me to live my life in full expression, with deep gratitude and compassion for human suffering that I otherwise would not have.**

If you are struggling through the depths of depression, it is essential that you take on the practice of self-compassion, starting today. Dr. Kristin Neff's book *Self-compassion: Stop Beating Yourself Up and Leave Insecurity Behind* identifies three components to self-compassion that I believe are a winning formula for any issue in our lives but are particularly helpful for dealing with any kind of mental illness:

1) **Self-kindness,** which is the ability to be warm and understanding toward ourselves when we suffer as opposed to using self-criticism.
2) **Common humanity**, which is cultivating the awareness that we are not alone in our suffering and that we all have moments when we feel inadequate.
3) **Mindfulness,** which is the ability to view a situation in a balanced way by acknowledging our negative feelings without exaggeration or becoming consumed by the pain.

With ancient wisdom and modern mindfulness techniques, we have a strong cache of resources to effectively deal with depression. While antidepressant medication may be necessary to augment one's recovery, with a 400% increase in prescriptions over the last decade, I think it's safe to say we are over medicating a condition that has been misunderstood for a very long time. What we could be focusing on are the factors that help us feel better naturally, such as loving intimate relationships, socialization, talk therapy, physical activity, time in nature, deep breathing, proper nutrition and spiritual connection, to name a few.

To healing, self expression and kindness to all,

Depression

Everyone experiences bouts of sadness once in a while, and we all experience grief from time to time. Depression, however, if left unaddressed, can develop into a life threatening medical condition that can consume someone's entire life, even leading to suicidal tendencies.

The following are nine symptoms that indicate clinical depression:
1) Depressed mood on most days and for most of each day.
2) Loss of pleasure in formerly pleasurable activities.
3) Significant increase or decrease in appetite, weight, or both.
4) Sleep problems, either insomnia or excessive sleepiness.
5) Feelings of agitation or a sense of intense lethargy
6) Loss of energy or excessive fatigue daily.
7) A persistent sense of guilt or worthlessness.

8) Inability to concentrate, occurring nearly every day.
9) Recurrent thoughts of death or suicide.

Research has identified three main brain chemicals, called neurotransmitters, that influence a depressive state; serotonin (our happy hormone that we feel in the presence of kindness or joy), norepinephrine (our stress hormone that drives us to respond in fight or flight), and dopamine (the pleasure chemical that lures us to the freezer for ice cream, or to the habit of chronically checking social media). When these chemicals are out of balance, our mood and eventually our temperament may become imbalanced as well.

For various reasons, medication is the primary treatment for depression today, and yet, there are other therapies for the mind and body that can assist a person in returning to their naturally balanced state of health and well-being. Medication in many cases may be necessary and useful, while at other times unnecessary, so these practices can work with or without prescribed medications.

The key in understanding depression and any other mental illness, is that it doesn't define who you are and is nothing to be embarrassed about.[30]

THREE TYPES OF DEPRESSION

Vata (Anxious) depression: the most common type of depression, especially in women, caused from inadequate supply of serotonin, from stress and our reaction to it that leads to chronic, or long term stress. Deficiencies in serotonin can cause us to become insecure, which can lead to reclusive behavior where we withdraw from life entirely. To feel better, we then reach for food, or substances to boost our mood, not realizing that this behavior can establish devastating and life threatening addictions.

Pitta (Agitated) depression: caused from chronic stress and over-scheduled lives, and the stimulants we consume to manage all that. This state of depression can be characterized as an edginess, irritation or angry mood, similar to the imbalanced state of the fire body/mind type. In this state, it can feel difficult to exhale, the mind is racing and movements are often quick and erratic. With a clenched fist, the body language is usually tense, with hardened muscles. In a type A personality, the fight/flight stress response switch can be permanently flicked on.

Kapha (Sluggish) Depression: is characterized by sluggishness, hopelessness, melancholy, lack of inspiration to get up and start the day, bouts of crying, no energy and feeling disempowered in one's life. Physically, a person may have droopy or sad eyes, slouched posture, rounded shoulders, shallow breathing, with a bland facial expression.

---

[30] Yoga Journal and Timothy McCall, *Yoga as Medicine* (Penguin Random House, 2007)

> Depression lies. It tells you you are worthless. Here is the truth. You have value. You have worth. You are loved. Trust the voice of those who love you. ~ Eleni Pinnow, whose sister, Aletha, committed suicide.

Yoga for Depression

Yoga helps to bypass the brain and draws us right into the heart. When we become present to the essence of the heart, we can begin to feel in order to heal. By moving the body in specific ways, we naturally balance chemicals within the brain and body. Renowned yoga instructor, Patricia Walden, reports how her life began to evolve from chronic depression when she learned to simply "open her armpits". This movement translated into opening her heart, which deepened her breath and reconnected her to the feeling tone of her emotions.

Did you know that it's normal to feel sad? Sadness is not a sign that something is wrong with you, nor is it something you need to rush to change or fix. Sadness is a natural feeling within the human experience. When sadness visits your life, it is a sign that a part of you deep inside needs your love and attention. Instead of moving away from your sadness by attempting to bury it or numb out, try softening around your sadness with pure presence. No drama, no stories, no fear, imagine if we all approached sadness with curiosity, open to receiving the sacred wisdom that lives within our pain?

Throughout this program, you can practice softening around *any* emotion that arises and just let it be present. Like a child in need of attention, it's when we ignore sensations and feelings that they tend to become louder and more persevering, calling out for attention. Give yourself the space here to just be present to yourself the emotional landscape of your life.

Why Optimism

> "Happiness is your nature. It is not wrong to desire it. What is wrong is seeking it outside when it is inside." Ramana Maharshi

Let's describe optimism by exploring it's opposite—pessimism. Pessimism is characterized by an attitude of doom, expecting the worst from life as it unfolds moment by moment. Pessimism breads fear, disappointment and a pressing need to control life situations. We all know that having full control over life is impossible so when the unexpected occurs, which it does, we feel intense frustration on top of fear and disappointment!

Optimism on the other hand, is the practice of looking for the good in life, not in a naïve way, but in a conscious way. Living naively would look like a person who blindly trusts that everyone's intentions are wholesome. Living optimally involves living with discernment, while believing that life is conspiring on our behalf, even in moments when we can't see the big picture. Choosing an optimistic attitude fortifies our faith in the goodness of the world, and the more goodness we focus on, the more we attract in our lives because we live in a magnetic universe. Have you ever noticed that what you focus on you receive more of in your life? If our perspective dictates our experience of life, it makes sense to examine the lens by which we view the world.

In terms of neuroscience, research shows that the practice of mindfulness (paying attention to the present moment in a neutral, non-judgmental way) helps us to cultivate traits such as happiness, optimism and compassion. This exciting new research shows that we can actually influence our temperament by being aware of our thoughts and guiding them constructively. Here's how it happens: when we have a thought, certain areas of the brain are activated. If we have repeated thoughts, we repeatedly activate the same area of the brain. This repetitive brain activity actually changes the structures of the brain itself, in other words, our thoughts actually shape of our brains, which then influences our future thoughts! You can see how a traumatic event, or a negative situation that caused us to feel sad, could eventually lead to chronic or clinical depression if the pattern is not intervened. On the flip side, we can be empowered by the knowledge that no matter what happens in life, with the right skills and support, we can always choose to heal and be happy, and we do this through the dedicated practice optimism. When life strikes, optimism calls us to look for the gift, like the single beautiful flower that grows out of the crack in a barren rock face. Optimism invites us to walk on the sunny side of life whenever possible by noticing the blessings in the moment. Optimism involves giving thanks for what we have, and giving more thanks and then giving thanks again, even when we're not feeling very fortunate.

One of the greatest stories of optimism can be found in Victor Frankl's Man's Search for Meaning; reflections on life in the Nazi concentration camp. His situation grew so desperate that at one point he was served rotten fish eyes for dinner. Knowing that he had to eat this to survive, he closed his eyes and envisioned a beautiful nourishing meal before him, allowing him to consume what was provided with gratitude. While most of his inmates died, he managed to survive through the undying optimism that his freedom was within reach.

If our thoughts then, influence the activity within our brains, what kind of structures are your building?

THE BODY SPEAKS YOUR MIND

Did you know that our body language influences our mood?

Did you know that the body influences our brain chemicals and by gaining mindfulness of how we position our bodies, we can enhance our mood, boosting healthy hormones and decreasing stress hormones?

It makes sense then to examine the language of our body so that we can choose body postures that shift depressive, disempowered energy into more uplifting states of mind and body.

Did you know that 90% of our communication is exchanged non-verbally? What you say with your body, intentionally or unintentionally, has a huge impact on your relationships and greatly affects how people perceive you in the world.

Studies show that the way we carry ourselves influences almost every aspect of our lives. Everyday we make instant judgments about people based on their body expressions and posture. And those judgments can determine really important life outcomes such as job opportunities, intimate relationships and friendships.

It's not just other people's judgments that count in life. Your own opinion of yourself is reflected through your body language all the time. And every posture has it's own biochemical influence on our whole system, so this is very empowering information for us!

Did you know that women who walk with confidence, head held high, are less likely to be assaulted than those demonstrating insecure body language?

"She unknowingly sent out signals that marked her as a 'soft' target." –when prisoners who had been convicted for assault were asked if there were certain people they would decide to attack "Those who walked with confidence were less likely to be assaulted."[31]

You may need to fake it 'til you make it, or as social scientist Amy Cuddy says "Fake it 'til you *become* it." We can do this by reflecting on the following suggestions:
- Identify the desired message you'd like to communicate to yourself and the world. How do you wish to be perceived by others? Write it down here:

_____

_____

The more clear you are about how you want to be seen, the easier it will be to describe the physical body language that matches your desired message. Describe your body language here:

_____

_____

- Try them out—let your body express the mental portrait you've just painted by exploring various postures that reflect your desired message.
- Continue exploring and "faking it" every day in different situations, until you naturally and authentically embody your desired message through the energy and attitude within you.

Low and high power postures

According to Cuddy, in the presence of a high-powered posture, we tend to do the opposite and shrink to balance it out. Is there a time in your life when you noticed yourself cower in the presence of a person with big, high-powered energy?

In terms of gender, it's no surprise that women tend to assume a low-powered posture in comparison to men. But we can be reassured to know that power postures aren't reliant on physical size and shape, otherwise most men would dominate every encounter.

What's most influential is our sense of self-worth (the relationship we have with ourselves), which is then conveyed as self esteem through our body language. Self-worth, self-esteem and the thoughts we think all affect our hormonal states and our energy levels, which contribute to the powerful messages we deliver to the world. We are all sending messages to the world around us through our body language, and most of us are doing this unconsciously. By becoming aware that our bodies reflect our internal state, we can then be more intentional about how we hold ourselves physically. Hopefully it's reassuring and exciting to learn that

---

[31] "Marked for Mayhem" *Psychology Today, Jan. 9, 2009,* https://www.psychologytoday.com/articles/200901/marked-mayhem

just as our thoughts influence our physical posture, our bodily posture can also affect how we think and feel about ourselves!

Every posture we do in the Girl on Fire Program is designed to support you in discovering unwavering confidence, centered awareness, grace and ease of embodiment.

If thoughts become our body language, we better choose our thoughts wisely!

"Choose to be optimistic, it feels better." Dalai Lama XIV

The power of a smile

It's true that our body posture makes a difference in how we feel and what we think, but did you know that a slight change in your facial expression can also lead to powerful shifts in your state of mind? Did you know that smiling can uplift your mood, even if it's a fake smile?

Have you ever noticed what happens when someone's telling a joke and they start smiling and giggling before the punch line? The people listening inevitably start laughing as well, because smiling is contagious.

On the flip side of this argument in favor of smiling, sometimes we use the smile to mask what's really going on inside. Have you ever faked a smile to conceal your true feelings? If there is an underlying issue that's been left unaddressed, such as trauma, grief or low self worth, you are encouraged to give it the attention it requires in order to heal, move on and be truly happy.

Here's some happy news:

Studies suggest that a simple smile, forced or natural, can decrease stress and uplift our mood by releasing happy hormones. Smiling apparently makes us more attractive, more approachable in a crowd and more trustworthy by helping others around us feel better. Additionally, smiling and laughter boost our immunity and our ability to fight off illnesses, even into the next day.

Inner Smile

Smiling is considered to be one of the secrets to long life, relieving stress and promoting happiness. When we smile we send a message to the body that we are feeling good. That's a pretty easy way of generating positive energy, isn't it?

Remember the practice of Pratipaksha Bhavana? It is the process by which we transform one state of energy into another, and a smile does the same thing. Like turning lead into gold, smiling transforms heavy energy into light energy by changing our body's feeling state from lethargic or depressed into a golden state of energy and aliveness.

While it may take a real effort to put a smile on your face if you're feeling really down, it is possible to shift negative energy into positive energy. After all, depressed energy is not bad or wrong, it's just a natural reaction to stress or trauma. But when it lingers, depression can become a state of being, dampening our inner flame and pulling us away from the stream of well-being.

With awareness, we can use the energy that may be going toward feeding depression and use it to grow happiness, contentment and joy. A smile helps us to take this depressed, sad or heavy energy and use it for our benefit.

"There are no language barriers when you are smiling." Allen Klein

A CALL TO MAKE A CHANGE

When we're outside of the stream of well-being, caused by either physical or mental misalignment, it is not bad or good. Without judgment, we can view this state of misalignment a call to tweak the way in which we're living and refine our lifestyle habits.

Take a moment in your journal to assess your life, and your approach to it, including your schedule, work, school, friends, stress levels, your thoughts and inner dialogue. If you notice that depression is a regular feeling state, record the factors that contribute to it.

Making changes to your life can be really scary, because doing anything we've never done before has elements of uncertainty and lack of control. But change can also be exciting and filled with possibility for improvement.

Shraddha, faith, is required for anyone on the yogic path, as we are called to surrender into the flow of life, to listen intently to our hearts, and follow the direction of our inner longings. Having faith that we are being guided by a Universal power greater than us, allows us to let go and trust the process of healing, while seeking help in our healing. With faith, we learn to approach life with optimism, expecting miracles and goodness.

"Sometimes your only available transportation is a leap of faith." Margaret Shepard

Energetically speaking, anxiety and depression can show up on opposite sides of the scale. With regards to anxiety, our energy can become trapped in the upper regions of the body as we hold our breath to manage the inner chaos. Depression on the other hand, can cause our energy to become stagnant in the lower regions of the body. Our work, as we know, with anxiety is to bring our energy down from the frantic thoughts in the mind into our lower chakras, which we do best through belly breathing and grounding practices. With the heavy and dark energy of depression, which can be a form of excessive kapha, we need techniques that will invigorate, uplift and circulate energy. Although our movement practices are different, the general recommendations are similar: exercise, fresh air, live your truth, find a creative outlet, discover a practice that fosters spiritual connection, deep breathing, friendship and community, meditation and self care. When we do yoga, or spend time with someone who fills our bucket or engage in a personal passion, we are fueling the spark of light within, leading us toward our highest Self, who is unstoppable, unbounded, free and strong.

OMWORK

Write a short story about your key interests and passions as a child, including any moments of clarity you had about what you were meant to do with your life (like Olympian Karen Furneaux, at age 10, telling her parents after watching the torch run that she would one day participate in the Olympic Games).

Interview friends and relatives if they recall speaking about their dreams, or if they recall a particular activity that they loved to do. Journal about your findings.

Affirmations

Today, I smile into the center of my being.

Today I give myself the gift of absorbing the uplifting energy of nature.

I commit in this moment to living with love, light, laughter and gratitude.

"Rule #1: Don't sweat the small stuff. Rule #2: It's all small stuff." R.S. Elliott

Personal addition:

Physical posture

Dancer Posture

Mindful Movement Class - Week 8

NOTE: This is the Mindful Movement Class to accompany Week 8. For consistency and ease, we recommend the video series of these classes available at www.GirlOnFire.ca.

Weekly theme – Optimism
Sukhasana/Easy Pose with Prana Mudra Savasana Apanasana/Knee to Chest Pose Mountain Pose Cleansing arm vinyasa Lions Breath Spinal Cord Breathing Turning the wheel, circulating a qi ball. Tiger Flow Arm Pumps with laughter Shake it out, add a smile Classical Namaskaras with affirmations Lion Climbing Mountain Lunges Windmill arm vinyasa **Feature Posture**: Dancer Pose **Partner Posture:** Partner Dancer Awakening Serpent Flow Half Locust Pose Downward Dog Pigeon Pose Knees to Chest Pose Savasana/Relaxation Pose
Girl on Fire closing To acknowledge the three centers of Power, Love and Insight: Rise to sitting and bring palms together. Lift hands so that thumbs touch the mid eye point and say: *"Guided by insight"* Now draw hands to heart, one palm on heart center in the middle of the chest and the other palm resting on top of the first hand and say: *"I listen to my heart's desire"* Now take the top hand and slide it down so it rests on the navel, with the first hand remaining on the heart and say: *"And take positive, powerful action in the world"*

Notes

Week 9 – Contentment

This week's focus is to gain deeper understanding of:
- Perfectionism vs. Love
- Addiction and your body
- Mistakes of the Intellect

A Message from Jenny

Perfectionism is referred to in Ayurveda as a pitta or fire body/mind trait. Being the strong pitta that I am, perfectionism and I have had a long-standing relationship. I have always been very particular about my appearance and my performance in the world. As a child, in my grade four year, I received a mere gold level on my Canadian fitness appraisal. I was so appalled by my less than perfect score that I spent the following year training to ensure I received the red excellence badge in grade five. While the seeds of perfectionism were there, they were matched by the healthy desire to give my very best coupled by the excitement of exploring my personal limits. By the time I entered high school, my desire to just be my best was superseded by the obsessive drive to be perfect.

Throughout high school, as my parent's relationship, along with my sense of security, eroded, my addiction to perfection grew. And as my addiction to perfection grew, so did my anxiety and fear of failure. I stopped playing the sports I was mediocre in, I refused opportunities in school musicals and became more obsessed with perfecting my performance in basketball. Before I knew it, my world had become very small, and very controlled. I unconsciously misplaced my value as a person, handing it over to the scoreboard and peer approval. By the end of my final year, I was engrossed in a perfection-addicted state. Although I was chosen as the most valuable player and recruited by three top Universities, I still found reasons to support my "not good enough" story.

So when basketball season had come to a close, I transferred my perfection addiction to my appearance, and went to work on becoming, not even having, but becoming, the "perfect body." In attempts to achieve this, my life became even more contracted. I stopped swimming for fear that someone might judge my body. I stopped wrestling with my siblings for fear that my make up would smudge. I stopped singing for fear that I might slide out of key. Pretty soon, I had relinquished all sources of enjoyment in my life in honor of perfection.

The prison of perfection came to a peak when I was 19, and still a virgin. I had been dating my first long term boyfriend for a year at Acadia, and I while I loved him, I was terrified of true intimacy. Without the graphic resources available today, and very little guidance from my superiors on how the whole sex thing panned out, I was consumed by the possibility that I might mess it up. What if my body didn't do what it was supposed to? I had no opportunities to practice beforehand and no way of refining my skills before the big event. It was like being thrown into a championship game, without a clue how to play!

In a state of overwhelm, I did my best to postpone the inevitable. When we chose to take a break from the relationship for the summer, I was determined to figure things out. Five days before my twentieth birthday, and my return to Acadia, I went out on the town with my girlfriends. At the Three Mile Beverage Room, a way too sleazy bar for a group of teen girls, I had a brief conversation with a gorgeous man I had seen at the gym all summer. He seemed nice enough, and most importantly, was a stranger for me to get this sex thing over with. In our brief conversation, I poured on the flirting in hopes of initiating some action. After too much to drink, I found myself waiting outside for the rest of my friends at the end of the night. He found me first and so off we went to his dingy apartment to do the deed. On a mattress minus sheets, with a photo of his very goth looking ex girlfriend on the dresser, he laid me down and did the merciful thing of having sex with me. After three short minutes, the show was over, and pizza was ordered. I left feeling thankful that the deed was 'done' but more confused than ever. If that's what sex is all about, why does it occupy so much of our attention and marketing dollars?

The next day, it hit me hard. I never predicted I would feel so empty. I just gave away the most sacred part of myself to a guy I'd likely never see again, all because I was afraid of being anything less than perfect. There was a strange need in me to see him one more time and my sister Lisa agreed to drive in town with me. Before I left the house, I ran into my room and grabbed a little teddy bear I had had for years. Off we went, in search of a stranger who had just taken my virginity. When we arrived, he was just packing his car to head west, to pursue a modeling career with Jockey underwear (I told you he was gorgeous). I wished him well and handed him the teddy that symbolized for me, the giving away of my childhood innocence. "What's this for?" he asked aloofly. "Just take it, please, just take it" I begged. His eyes grew wide as he asked, "That wasn't your first time?" I jumped into the car and drove away, saving myself from having to admit the painful and humiliating truth that I chose a quick, cold exchange with a stranger over a tender expression of love with a man I adored.

It is clear to me now that perfectionism came from my inherent lack of self worth, and I made the painful mistake of expecting it to fill my desperate need for love. Unfortunately, this perspective only proved to deepen the void within me instead of filling it.

If you share the same addiction to perfection, know that life truly begins when you choose to give it up. What's helped me escaped from this prison is keeping my inner flame well stoked with love and that requires me to choose people in my life who fuel my flame, not squelch it. Also, as I write this I have a stuffed Olaf beside me to remind me to laugh and take my life lightly, because I know that if I don't, I can easily become paralyzed by perfection and nothing gets completed.

And as Superhero Andrea Scher, award winning blogger says "Perfection is the enemy of done. Good enough is really darn good."

Amen,

Jenny

Perfectionism vs Love

> It's better to live your own life authentically and to do it imperfectly, than to live someone else's life, perfectly. ~ Bhagavad Gita

Fixed versus Growth Mindset

When we strive for perfection, we're caught in the web of what Carol Dweck, (author of *Mindset: the new Psychology of Success*) calls a fixed mindset. According to Dweck, a fixed mindset believes that our basic intelligence and creative abilities are unchanging factors that we can't really change. The fixed mindset believes that our success in life is predetermined by our level of intelligence (that does not change) and how it measures up to an equally fixed standard. Therefore, striving for success and avoiding failure at all costs becomes the way of maintaining one's sense of being smart or skilled. A fixed mindset is affirmed when you are told you succeeded or not, because of your innate intelligence. This mindset is based on a need to appear smart, and therefore leads to: jealousy and competition, fear of criticism, viewing effort as hard work, giving up easily when faced with obstacles and avoiding challenges that may threaten the image that you've worked so hard to create. Can you see how a fixed mindset, along with an unstable self-worth leads to perfectionism tendencies?

Week 9 – Contentment

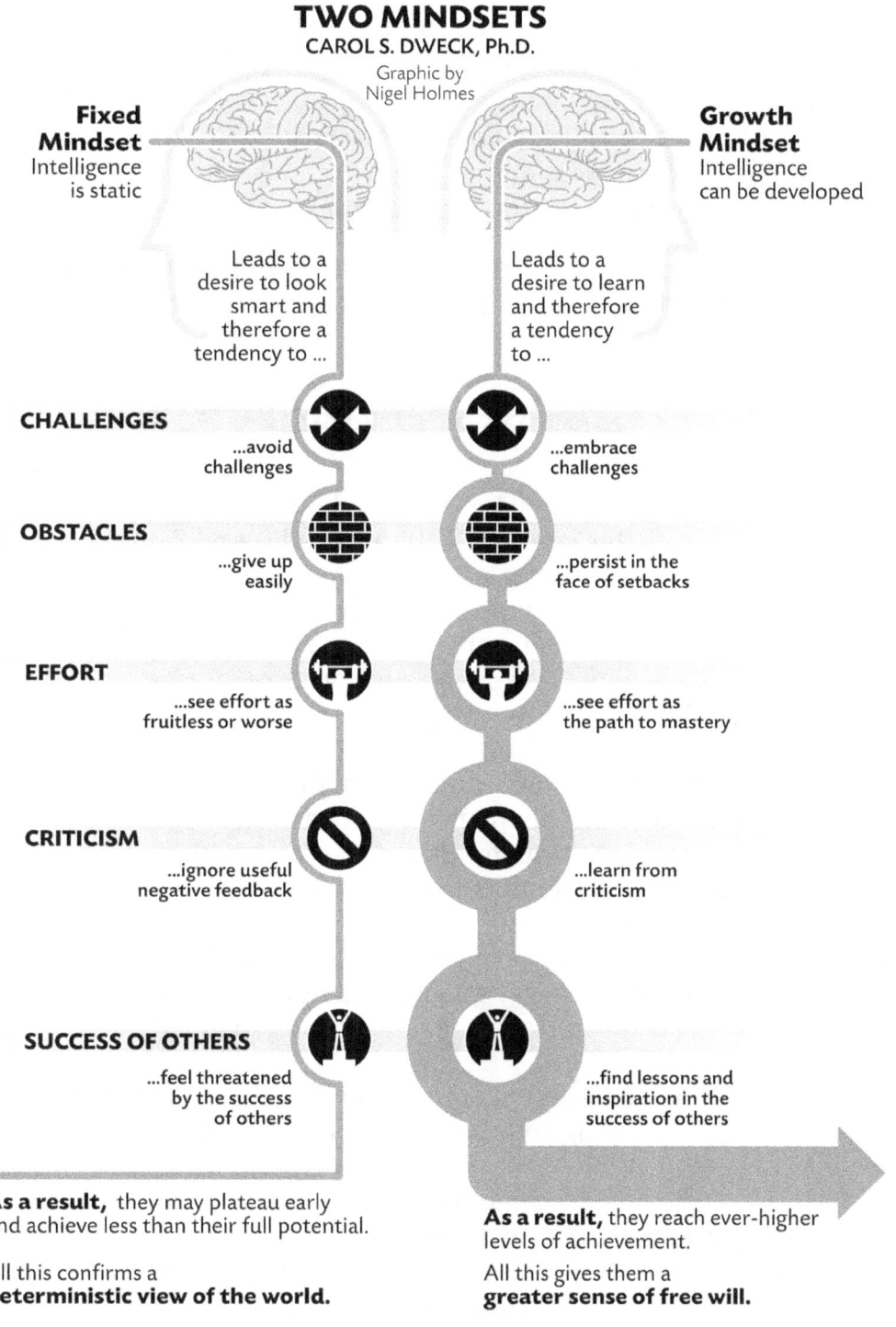

http://nigelholmes.com/graphic/two-mindsets-stanford-magazine/

A growth mindset on the other hand, is where the magic happens. This mindset thrives on challenge and sees failure as an invitation for further growth, not as evidence of one's inability. At the core of a growth mindset is the belief that hard work and drive can indeed affect your intelligence and your success in life. This mindset is based on a desire to grow and be one's best. When you assume a growth mindset you:
- gain inspiration from others' success,
- learn from criticism,
- view effort as a necessary ingredient for mastery
- persist in the face of setbacks and
- embrace challenges as part of the growth process.

Doesn't that sound different from the fixed mindset? The growth mindset sets us free to fall down, make mistakes and explore our limits, knowing that we are ever expanding beings of infinite potential.

SEEK WHOLENESS, NOT PERFECTION!

Here's the real truth about perfectionism: no one, not even super models or celebrities, can achieve perfection (although they often pull off the façade of perfection), nor are we supposed to achieve it, because perfection is not a human possibility. The human condition requires imperfection and yes, failure in order for us to grow into the beautiful, wise, powerful beings we are born to be. Singer, songwriter Beth Neilson Chapman once said in a concert, "There are no mistakes   just variations." Through this work, you are being given opportunities to assess the way in which you're living your life, with the hope that you can find the key to your perfectionism prison and let yourself out.

The Greek word for perfect is whole, referring to the perfection of who we are at our core. Babies are the embodiment of this divine perfection, and they spend all their time being, not doing anything at all! Our work through this process of waking up is to commit to becoming whole and abandon the useless attempts to achieve outward perfection, which only wastes our precious time here on earth.

No longer confined by unrealistic expectations, you can allow the real you to live your life fully and as you do that, creative energy and joy will flow through you. And the next time you make a mistake? The bigger the mistake, the louder you can laugh!

> You could spend the rest of your life in the straight jacket of perfection,
> Primping your hair and make up in the mirror
> Or
> You could fully experience life,
> Letting yourself fall down and get dirty, messy, and real.
> Splash through the mud on your bike and eat sticky marshmallows.
> What path will you choose?

What would your life look like if you dropped the burden of perfection?
What would you have to let go of to accept this new self?
What activities might you try that you've avoided out of fear of not being perfect?

Addiction

Addiction comes from the Latin word meaning "bonded" and is defined as anything that brings pleasure but has long-term negative consequences. By this definition, most of the human population struggles with addiction in some form. Addiction can be viewed as an unskillful attempt to get a love need met. In fact, addicts often describe the feeling of being high as a warm loving hug because it releases endorphins, opiates in the brain that are also released in the presence of love. When our love needs aren't met as children, or if we survived trauma, addiction is a common—yet unskillful—way of getting that need met. As we know from previous sessions, working with the 3A's (admit, allow and act), and having the courage to admit and identify the painful pattern is the first big step in the healing process. We have previously viewed addiction involving a substance but we can most certainly become addicted to perfection and the striving of it.

Body Perfect

Perfectionism is one of the main causes of stress for women and we have been trained to strive for perfection through the media that promises happiness in physical perfection. With the unrealistic standards of airbrushed models and celebrities who undergo untold plastic surgeries, it's no wonder we've become self-obsessed and body addicted in a desperate attempt to measure up. But as we withdraw our attention from the destructive and abusive media influences around us, we gradually learn to rely more on our inner treasures that bring lasting peace and contentment. Despite the messages you've been inundated with, the purpose of your life is far more important than physical perfection. In fact, the purpose of life has very little to do with your body at all! The trouble with perfectionism is that it's an impossible goal that will never be achieved so it inevitably leads us back into the cycle of anxiety and eventual despair.

The media has attempted to disempower the feminine by making her thin, without curves, dry, lifeless, without passion, without menses, unable to birth, dressed up in heels and tight clothing, unable to walk (let alone run) freely, unable to breathe and feel fully. Culturally, we have squelched the feminine with the pressure to be perfect physically, academically, athletically, professionally, etc. And this pressure has increased our sense of competition with other women, creating separation with other women who might otherwise be our greatest allies. As we continue to climb the proverbial ladder, our brain construction is changing and so are our hormones. As a result of striving for perfection, testosterone, which we all have in varying degrees, is increasing, making us more aggressive and driven. We need the balance of the female hormones, namely estrogen and progesterone, for self-nourishment and for being kind and compassionate women in the world.

If the female breast is the proverbial symbol of nourishment, it's no wonder cancer of the breast has become the epidemic that it is. We are socialized to put others before our own needs in order to be the perfect partner, or mother or employee, and as a result we fail to properly nourish ourselves. This unique western approach to life is counter to the eastern traditions that emphasize the importance of nurturing our life force energy and living with balance. We know that too many years of pushing ourselves to the limit will cause burn out, adrenal fatigue and disease. Yes, we can be ambitious, driven change agents in the world, we just need to do that in a way that is respectful of our stream of wellbeing. Now is a great time for you to be considering how you want to live your life, before you enter your adult years.

Contentment, or *Santosha*, is an inner treasure that most spiritual traditions encourage, as it stands in opposition to the drive for perfection and success. Striving takes a great deal of energy and often breeds anger and resentment when things don't go as planned. When we have an ideal outcome in our minds and strive to fulfill that exact and vision of perfection, our lives become fixed, rigid and inflexible. This leads to the feeling of unrest, reflective of a lack of peace.

The Dalai Lama claimed that the definition of misery is the state of wanting to be someone other than who you are. You were born into the family you have for a reason. You were born with the gifts and challenges you have for a reason. You were born with the unique body you have, for a reason. Your work in this lifetime is NOT to spend your precious life energy trying to be someone else. Your job is to accept who you are, and then work toward becoming as fully you as you can be. And in yogic terms, that's contentment!

You are invited here to replace your driving need for perfection with the inner treasure of contentment, the practice of being content with what you have and who you are in this moment. Although the media touts the opposite message, the real truth is that more is not always better; in fact, more can bring great stress and complexities. By cultivating contentment, we let go of the illusion that life will be better when our dreams come true. We relax into the peaceful now, letting go of the neurotic cultural pattern of always wanting what we don't have and instead, choosing to want what we have.

The path of peace and contentment that a Girl on Fire walks is about radical self-love, true and total acceptance of who you really are, without changing anything in this moment. Once we've given ourselves that gift of acceptance, we then commit to continuing our growth as a person, because that's what we do as living, breathing creatures. We are not meant to just succumb to mediocrity but to strive for our highest potential, while loving our imperfections.

Write an affirmation on acceptance of yourself, just as you are in this moment. You are worthy of taking up space in this world. You are worthy of respect from others, because you are a spark of the same brilliant flame that created the entire Universe. Make the commitment today to start loving yourself, for no one else can fully appreciate you until you appreciate yourself. No one else can truly love you until you love yourself. No one else can deeply respect you, until you respect yourself.

Mistake of the Intellect

There is an Ayurvedic principle called "mistake of the intellect." You may have mistakenly learned that you have to look or be perfect to be accepted in society. When we subscribe to external standards, we are living according to the false self, the self that is not us, because we are not just the body, nor the mind/intellect, we are the self—the soul within and it is always guiding us, we just need to enter the quiet, still space within to listen for its guidance. There are a million radio stations you could be tuning into and your work is to tune your radio to the station that affirms your true brilliant self.

Behind the mistake of the intellect is the truth that we are here to love our selves and others; everything else is just an opportunity for deeper understanding of ourselves that can circle us back to the core of our being, which is love. Learning to love and live fully is truly your greatest work in this lifetime. The other path, like the path of perfection, striving, anger, competition and jealousy might be the most common route but it is a reflection of the lowest, most unconscious part of ourselves. While it's easy, it's also painful and lonely.

True happiness and contentment come from tapping into the abundant Love Intelligence that is always advocating for our highest potential. The path of love can be difficult though because it forces us to grow, and be accountable for our non-loving actions. The path of love is the path of immense courage, and it is undoubtedly the road less travelled. By committing to the path of love, you are taking a brave step toward becoming your greatest self, and being a true light bearer, a Girl on Fire.

Omwork

Pillowcase Painting

Using affirmations, mantras or symbols that inspire, create a pillowcase that reflects the concepts discussed in this or previous classes to support a deep and peaceful sleep. Examples:
- I am so lovable!
- Sweet Dreams Beautiful!
- I'm following my dreams!
- I am amazing!
- Tomorrow is *my* day!

Affirmations

I have the opportunity to create the most authentic version of who I am, now.

I choose to view mistakes as an important step on the way to becoming the best I can be!

I am whole and complete, healthy and happy, just as I am.

Today, I seek wholeness, not perfection!

Personal additions:

Physical posture

Goddess Posture and/or Kidney Flow

Mindful Movement Class - Week 9

NOTE: This is the Mindful Movement Class to accompany Week 9. For consistency and ease, we recommend the video series of these classes available at www.GirlOnFire.ca.

Weekly theme – Contentment
Supine Bound Angle Pose with Yoni Mudra, set intention   Seated Sufi Grind   Fire Breathing   **Feature Posture:** Table to Goddess Pose (foot stretch)   Downward Dog with wave   Neck stretches   **Partner Posture:** Standing Twist   Shoulder shrugs   **Feature Posture:** Kidney Flow   Standing Spinal Wave   Horse Stance with Yoni Mudra   Rag Doll with Fall Out Breaths   Yogic Squat to Forward Bend vinyasa   Phoenix Pose   Mandala Namaskara: this namaskara flows in a complete circle, first counter clockwise, then clockwise, returning back to the beginning orientation on our mats.   This sequence beautifully blends the opposite energies of life that we strive to balance through our practice; strength and power with flexibility and suppleness. Stay with your breath and follow the intelligence of your own energy flowing through you, it will guide you to body freedom and inner balance.   1) Downward dog   2) Inhale lift right leg and open hip   3) Exhale step it through and turn to right, coming to outer border of right and left foot with left hand anchored   4) Sweep right arm forward and back 3x   5) Move in the direction of the left side now, skandasana over left leg, right leg straight   6) Face the back of the mat in a lunge, back knee dropped, interlock last three fingers and stretch arms overhead   7) Exhale slide left leg back into plankasana, to cobra to downward dog, facing back of mat   8) Inhale right leg up again, exhale step it through, repeating step 3-7, finishing facing the front of the mat.   9) Repeat sequence leading with the left leg.   10) Repeat both sides 1 to 2 more times.

Child's Pose
Supine Pigeon Pose
Savasana/Relaxation Pose

Girl on Fire closing

To acknowledge the three centers of Power, Love and Insight:

Rise to sitting and bring palms together. Lift hands so that thumbs touch the mid eye point and say: *"Guided by insight"*

Now draw hands to heart, one palm on heart center in the middle of the chest and the other palm resting on top of the first hand and say: *"I listen to my heart's desire"*

Now take the top hand and slide it down so it rests on the navel, with the first hand remaining on the heart and say: *"And take positive, powerful action in the world"*

Notes

Week 10 – Connection

This week's focus is to gain deeper understanding of:
- Kindness
- Conscious communication
- The 5 A's
- Sisterhood

KINDNESS

Despite our efforts to stand up against bullying, racial conflict and war, the unfortunate reality is that we are still treating one another harshly, often without regard for others' feelings. Many of us do not consider the lasting harm that we're inflicting on others with our unkind words, actions or even thoughts. We are all too quick to join in on gossip and conversations that are filled with judgment, criticism and cruelty. What's more, for many of us who are brought up in negative environments, we assume this way of being is normal. It might feel normal if you're familiar with negativity and conflict, but it's not healthy for anyone.

The exciting possibility is that your sense of self and core strength may be so well-established now that you no longer need to condemn or put down others to feel okay inside. It actually works the opposite anyway. Being nasty may feel good in the moment, as negative energy is released and directed at someone other than you, but its temporary because what we send out in the world is exactly what we receive back. Yup, life is like a boomerang that is thrown into the air and makes its way back to the one who threw it.

The words we speak and actions we take affect our own lives in very real and profound ways. If you speak, act and think negatively all day long, what energy do you think you are you exposing yourself to? Not the good stuff, that's for sure. And just because your family lives a certain way, or your friends talk a certain way, or the lyrics of your music sound a certain way, does not give you license to contribute to the cycle of pain that we all struggle with. You are worthy of more than that, shoot higher, go bigger, because the rewards of kindness and living in the light are so much greater!

Ultimately kindness is the practice of expanding your focus beyond you and your world to the awareness that everyone is living with their own brand of suffering. This awareness can change the way you react to just about everyone and everything in your life. Living mindfully, in a way that encourages us to pause, breathe and gather more information before reacting emotionally, can profoundly help us in being more kind to others.

The questions we can ask ourselves before we press send, or react verbally is:

"What reaction will this action cause?

"What kind of energy do I want in my life?"

Do you want strife and drama or peace and harmony? While sometimes it's important to set boundaries and speak our truth, there are many instances where we could give ourselves two or three hours, or longer before returning a text or phone call. Remember that when we're emotionally charged, our limbic system is lit up, not our reasoning mind. This is what causes regretful moments after the fact, when our emotional flames have settled and we can see the situation more clearly.

Living mindfully gives us the breathing space we need to step away from an inflamed situation, to take a walk in nature, or call a friend for a second opinion, or do some journaling so that we don't injure others with our own personal triggers.

Do you want to grow flowers with your life or are you unconsciously planting poison ivy? Whatever seeds we lay down in the past from our behavior, will determine the harvest that we will inevitably receive in our future.

Imagine what the world would be like if we, as a global community, understood that we are all one, we are all intricately connected and that we are all equally worthy of respect and love? The Golden Rule is a simple phrase that can be a guiding principle for our lives as Girl's on Fire: do unto others, as you would have them do unto you. As yogis, we are advised to consider the implications of our behavior before taking action, knowing that we can't take back the effects of a harsh word, or a hateful deed. We can only live through the consequences, which will match the vibration of the deed itself.

In every moment of our lives, we have the opportunity to spread love and positivity, or to cause pain and harm. We all know that fire misused or untamed can wreak havoc and devastate an environment. We also know that the discovery of fire has completely and positively transformed the human experience, bringing warmth and nourishment, light and energy. Now that you are conscious of the power of your inner flame, you must be aware of the Girl on Fire legacy you are now a part of, which is to:

- Use your fire to burn away negativity, suffering and cruelty both within yourself and the world around you
- Use your light to illuminate the darkness of ignorance (or not knowing) within yourself and the world around you
- Shine fully with the innate gifts you've been given, which inspires others to do the same

Through the ancient practice of yoga, we learn that the highest and most inspiring human behavior is demonstrated through kindness. We also know from the most current studies on brain science, that kindness makes everyone feel good, really good. And isn't that what we're all searching for?

Did you know that when a person does a random act of kindness, both the giver and the receiver of that kindness are flooded with feel good sensations caused by happy hormones called endorphins? What's more, did you know that acts of kindness are so powerful that even those who observe the exchange also receive a burst of positivity? If you find it difficult to break the habit of being nasty, take heart. It requires disciplined effort to change any ingrained habit but some simple changes in your life can support you in taking this new path.

What are some changes you can make in your life that will support you in becoming more

gentle, kind and ultimately more healthy within your relationships?
  Suggested answers:
- Seek therapy for issues of resentment that need forgiving
- Listen to inspiring music and TED Talks
- Read positive books
- Monitor media consumption, including social media and certain news stories
- Spend time with other girls on fire who share the same intentions
- Share your commitments with family members
- Propose to start, or augment, a school wide initiative on kindness, respect and equality

Like a candle lighting up a darkened room, our flame may not be huge, but when we let it shine, the whole world receives a portion of it. If Gandhi could ignite a nationwide revolution with a fierce commitment to non-violence, imagine what we can do together?

A Message from Jenny

A few years ago I was studying with Deepak Chopra and David Simon in California. After a week long intensive, I arrived at the airport and lugged my heavy suitcase to customs. Knowing I was well over my weight limit with the many books I had purchased, I stuffed as many as I could into my carry on. In light of my suspiciously heavy bag, the security man asked to open my bag. When he flipped it open, Deepak's image smiled up at us, as my books sprawled out onto the counter. The moment the man saw Deepak's face, his eyes lit up and got misty.
  "You know this man?" I asked.
  "Oh yes, Dr. Chopra comes through here a lot. He is such a nice man!"
  "I know what you mean, a pretty special human being indeed" I agreed.
  "Yeah, as busy as this place is, he always manages to leave us feeling better somehow. Seeing his face again just made my day. Thank you!"
  And off I went, grateful for the distraction from the weight of my bag. But more importantly, I was moved by this airport employee's reaction to a frequent traveler.
  Here is Deepak Chopra, famous spiritual teacher to many celebrities and politicians (and confidant to people like the late Michael Jackson), taking time to share his light with passing strangers on his path.
  This level of impact is what's possible when we commit to being love and spreading kindness!

The Rainbow Story

Author Unknown

This story emphasizes empowerment and sisterhood. The Universe is abundant and all our dreams can be fulfilled through cooperation and support.

Once upon a time the colors of the world started to quarrel. They all claimed that they were the best, the most important, the most useful, the favorite one.

Green said: "Clearly I am the most important. I am the sign of life and of hope. I was chosen for grass, leaves and trees. Without me, all animals would die. Look out over the countryside and you will see that I am the dominant shade."

Blue interrupted, "You only think about the Earth, but consider the sky and the sea. It is the water that is the basis of life, drawn up by the clouds from the deep sea. The sky gives space and peace and serenity. Without my peace, you would all be nothing."

Yellow chuckled, "You are all so serious. I bring laughter, joy and warmth to the world. The sun is yellow, the moon is yellow and the stars are yellow. Every time a sunflower blossoms the whole world smiles. Without me, there would be no fun."

Orange began to blow her temper, "I am the color of health and strength. I may be scarce but I am precious for I serve the needs of human life. I carry the most important vitamins. Think of carrots, pumpkins, oranges, mangos and papayas. I don't hang around all the time, but when I fill the sky at sunrise or sunset, my beauty is so striking that no one gives another thought to any of you."

Red could stand it no longer and she shouted out, "I am the ruler of all of you. I am blood! Life's blood. I am the color of danger and of bravery. I am willing to fight for a cause. I bring fire to the blood! I am the color of passion and of love, the red rose, the poppy and the poinsettia. Without me, the earth would be as empty as the moon!"

Purple rose to her full height. She was very tall and spoke with great clarity, "I am the color of royalty and power. Queens, chiefs, and bishops have always chosen me for I am a sign of authority and wisdom. People do not question me. They obey."

Finally, **Indigo** spoke, much more quietly than all the others but with just as much determination, "Consider me. I am the color of silence. You hardly notice me, but without me, you all become superficial. I represent thought and reflection, twilight and deep water. You need me for balance and contrast, for prayer and inner peace."

And so all the colors went on boasting and vying for their own superiority. Soon, their quarreling became louder and louder. Suddenly there was a startling flash of bright lightening! Thunder rolled and boomed! Rain started to pour down relentlessly. The colors crouched down in fear drawing close to one another for comfort.

In the midst of the clamor, a pure white light emerged from the lightning and began to speak, "You silly colors, fighting amongst yourselves, each trying to dominate the rest. Don't you know you were each made for a special purpose, unique and different? Join hands with one another and come to me." Doing as they were told, the colors united and joined hands. The white light continued: "From now on, worry not about who is the best and the brightest. Instead, focus on your special role within the universe. The next time it storms, each of you will stretch across the sky in a great bow of colors to remind the world of beauty, peace and the great miracle of life. We are here to bring hope for tomorrow, by shining together."

And so, in the future, whenever rain washes over the earth and a rainbow appears in the sky, let us remember what our special purpose is and appreciate one another.

Conscious communication

> In everyone's life at some time our inner fire goes out. It is then burst into flames by an encounter with another human being. We should all be thankful for those people who rekindle inner spirit. ~ Quote attributed to Albert Schweitzer

Competition and comparisons create separation and separation can lead to feelings of depression and isolation. Celebrating our gifts, and collaborating with other like-minded, heart-centered people give us life, energy, passion and joy. Women are wired for connection. We restore our happy hormones and do our best work when we connect with other women in a healthy and positive way.

The Five A's

The Five A's are known as our basic needs for thriving in the world:
Attention
Appreciation
Affection
Acceptance
Allowing

To communicate and connect with others effectively, we need to be able to enter that space, outside of our own ego bubble of the "I, me, mine" reality. Outside of that bubble is the space where we connect to others, which we can only do when we are truly present and intent on listening. Only then we can really hear what the other person is saying. When we enter that space in our awareness, true authentic connection can be made and all five A's can be satisfied.

Ways we communicate that create separation:
- Mock, or make fun of another
- Criticize another
- Divide your attention
- Ignore another
- Draw the conversation back to you

Ways we communicate that create connection:
- Listen with compassion and intent to understand
- Make eye contact
- Stay present
- Let them share without pulling the conversation to your experience

SISTERHOOD DECLARATION

Sisterhood is about honoring the Spirit in one another, not about the outer trappings of a person.
Sisterhood is about connecting through love, not about being right.
Sisterhood is about listening from the heart, not about analyzing with the head.
Sisterhood is about unconditional acceptance, not about judgment.
Sisterhood is about wildly celebrating each others' successes, not about competing for the best.
Sisterhood is about walking beside each other, it's not about leading.
Sisterhood is about 'being' together, not about the frantic need to 'do' something.
Sisterhood is about supporting one through struggle, without the need to fix her problems.
Sisterhood is about being present to one's pain, not about removing it.
Sisterhood is about sharing joy and laughter in all moments, not about waiting for life to align itself perfectly.
Sisterhood is about sharing the light of your soul with another sister, and witnessing your flames blazing as one, as they light up the night's sky.

Jenny Kierstead

OMWORK

Mentor under an inspiring person by assisting them in their work for a week. Examine their happiness, compassion and contribution.
    Write about these traits in your journal.

AFFIRMATIONS

Today, I bravely stand in opposition to negativity and choose to be an expression of kindness to all.

I live my life guided by my commitment to spreading goodness.

Today, I choose to make healthy, respectful relationship connections because I'm worth it.

With respect, I bow to the light within everyone.

Personal additions:

PHYSICAL POSTURE

Partner or solo Warrior 2 Posture

Mindful Movement Class - Week 10

NOTE: This is the Mindful Movement Class to accompany Week 10. For consistency and ease, we recommend the video series of these classes available at www.GirlOnFire.ca.

Weekly theme – Connection
Prana flow with hands at heart Partner Back-to-Back Breathing Pose—notice what it's like when someone's 'Got your back'. Seated Partner Twist Partner Side Stretch Interlock arms and press up to standing, using each other as support to rise. Temple Pose: face one another, pressing forearms together, lower torso with a flat back. Partner squat: facing one another, grab hold of each others forearms and lean away, then add a squat. **Feature Posture:** Partner Warrior 2 Partner Tree Pose Double Downward Dog Seated partner Wide Legged Forward Fold Buddy Boat Pose Lizard on a rock pose Seated Sukhasana with knees touching, take time for mindful stillness... "Not the ones speaking the same language, but the ones sharing the same feeling understand each other." Rumi Savasana/Relaxation Pose
Reflection Sacred Circle - read the Sisterhood Declaration
Girl on Fire closing To acknowledge the three centers of Power, Love and Insight: Rise to sitting and bring palms together. Lift hands so that thumbs touch the mid eye point and say: *"Guided by insight"* Now draw hands to heart, one palm on heart center in the middle of the chest and the other palm resting on top of the first hand and say: *"I listen to my heart's desire"* Now take the top hand and slide it down so it rests on the navel, with the first hand remaining on the heart and say: *"And take positive, powerful action in the world"*

NOTES

Week 11 – Essence

This week's focus is to gain deeper understanding of:
- Your essence and life purpose

A Message from Jenny

My older brother best dealt with my anorexia by withdrawing. A man of few words, he approached me one day in my final few months at Acadia, and asked in his logical way "Jenny how are you going to fulfill your dream of being a teacher in the state you're in?" Although his question shocked me, and frankly pissed me off a bit, I went away and did some deep thinking. Up until that point, I was solely consumed in my own suffering, but he was right. There was no way I could make a positive impact on anyone's life in the state I was in. Before I could even think about contributing to the world, I needed to discover who I was really was.

My life as I knew it was coming to a close and I knew I couldn't sustain the lifestyle I was living for much longer. Something brave inside me took a leap of faith and I asked myself "If I could do anything at all, what would I do?" The answer that came out was as surprising as the question. "I would work out west in the rocky mountains, of course" is what sang out from my heart. Where did that come from, I wondered? I had never been outside of the Maritimes, and had only seen the odd photo of the Rockies, like the lake on the back of the twenty-dollar bill. But crazily, I felt called, and I was determined to listen to the inner guidance that I had silenced for so long.

When I received the letter in the mail inviting me to spend the summer at Moraine Lake Lodge (yes, the very lake that was once featured on the Canadian twenty dollar bill), I knew this was the first step that would lead me out of this dark cloud I'd lived under for so many years.

My job description as a hiking guide was to develop an interpretive hiking service for guests. This invitation was the result of my new focus, which was to reclaim my essence. Sure enough, the gifts that were to follow helped open my eyes to the real and beautiful me.

My sister Lisa was also in a state of flux and ready for a new experience. We applied to a company that drove cars across the country and got a contract to drive an old brown dodge from Toronto to Calgary. That was a beautiful trip that gave us time to reconnect after our years away at separate universities. As we drove across the country, we raced trains along the Prairies, drove to the point of delirium, and had fits of laughter over what seemed an exciting prospect of being stopped by the police.

It was particularly healing for us to share the brokenness of our teen years, the pain that my illness caused her and the understanding we'd both come to over our parents' divorce. For the first time in a very long time, I cried and cried and cried. And then I laughed and laughed and laughed.

As we drove up the winding road, past Lake Louise toward Moraine Lake Lodge, I peered up with a gaping jaw at the peaks of the most magnificent mountains I had ever encountered. I knew, I just knew that the Universal Love Intelligence had positioned me here to blow my mind with her majesty. And she had already succeeded.

I spent the first few weeks of my summer working with park wardens to learn the history and flora and fauna of this foreign land. I guided visitors from all over the world through alpine trails. Each morning, my fellow pilgrims and I would begin at the base of the mountain and hike up switchbacks through an evergreen forest to eventually emerge above the tree line. There was beautiful symbolism here as just two months prior, I was wrestling with the shadow of life threatening patterns, and now, I was up in the peaks of mountains, gazing out over some of the most spectacular views in the world. I was returning to my early childhood of being immersed in the natural world, and my whole being began to align with the vibrant essence of Mother Nature. At times, my experience in the Rockies was beyond what my mind could conceive. Stepping outside my little cabin each morning to gaze at the panoramic view brought tears of awe and wonder.

I realized that summer, the important role that nature played in my healing. My senses began to awaken from their deep slumber, as I listened to the musical and uplifting sounds of the forest. The smells of sap and damp moss filled my nostrils. The fresh mountain air expanded my lungs like opening the windows of a cottage that had been closed for many seasons.

Being immersed in this natural environment helped me to revive my sense of spontaneity, adventure and play. We slept out under the stars at the far end of the lake, gazing up at the peaks in the moonlight. We went cycling through Banff on tandem bikes and did cartwheels on the top of the Tower of Babel. I was beginning to reconnect with the child inside who felt loved, whole and safe in the world. Happiness and contentment were seeping their way back into my soul.

I still struggled with the need to control and monitor my food intake, despite the miles and miles of hiking I did a day. Over time, I noticed the healthy me was starting to speak in a stronger, more confident voice. This was occurring naturally, as a byproduct of being away from the birthplace of my scars and doing what I loved, which was teaching and aligning with the intelligence and beauty of nature. I also noticed that my body's natural rhythms for things such as sleep, food and rest were re-establishing themselves.

Returning to nature also brought me back to my innate sense of playfulness. My microscopic mindset that obsessed about fear of failure and perfectionism began to dissolve. I was shifting from what Carolyn Myss calls a crisis of the first chakra, a perspective of humiliation of oneself, to seeing the sacred alive within me. Seeing the spark of the divine within myself was a significant awakening.

One of my greatest insights was discovering how important beauty was in order for me to thrive in my life. Not only beauty in my surroundings, but also within me. I yearned to feel beautiful on the inside, and be a living example of beauty in the world, in a flowing, glowing and vibrant kind of way -- not in a perfect, skinny, runway kind of way.

Surrounded by such natural beauty, I realized that if nature alone could create such a masterpiece as these mountains, then maybe, just maybe, I was a part of that design.

I AM SHAKTI

I am the creative, animating force within all life forms.
I freely express my elation and joy for being alive.
I am the one running wild with the animal kingdom.
I am the one swimming with the ocean currents.

With razor sharp instincts and intuitive wisdom,
I rage fiercely to right the wrongs,
And hold the wounded tenderly when love is lost.
My presence casts light on the soul's dark shadows,
Healing the ailment of illusion.

I am the shining one with the luminous flame,
Guiding you out of the fog of fear,
Calling you to live boldly on your terms
By moving in the direction of your true purpose.

With one glance, my light can alter your life forever,
And you can find me within the center of your being,
Where the power of the Universe pulses.
I am the one who provokes your growth,
I am the one who envelops you in love,
I am Shakti.

YOUR ESSENCE

In yoga we speak about the practice of uniting body, mind and spirit. Your essence is the part of your being that is both human and spiritual, it's invisible, without form and yet it is the true container of your life. Being the visual creatures that we are, we tend to assume that the body is most important in our lives. Though it does allow us to experience sensory life in human form, the body has its limitations. Imagine someone you love dearly without an essence, without the unique energy that makes them who they are? People without an essence would be mechanical robot type creatures wouldn't they? Life would be a vast, dull, uniform and boring landscape.

Our essence is more than just one part of the triad that makes us who we are. It surrounds and pervades the body. The body is the vehicle that houses and expresses our essence. But nor can our essence be confused as part of the mind. The wise nature of our essence has a different kind of knowing than the mind, with its random stream of thoughts and judgments. Your mind, like the body, has limits, whereas your essence is an infinite expanse of possibility.

Your essence is a brilliant inner light, a spark from the great flame of the Universe. Your essence is the unique radiance that inspires comments like, "Wow, she glows with beauty and happiness."

Have you ever noticed that everyone loves babies and even perfect strangers will reach out to touch them? When we are first born, we are more spiritual than we are human, and our essence is in full expression. As we grow, we become more self-conscious and cautious, and we veil our essence in an attempt to protect ourselves from harsh criticisms and ridicule. It's a bit funny that we spend the first part of our lives (especially our teen years) learning new skills and developing protective patterns, only to spend the second half of our lives unlearning and softening our protective layers so that we can shine fully and truly offer the gifts we've been given. There a few enlightened beings who skip past the instinct to conceal their true essence, but most of us require much encouragement to let our light shine.

Often when a person is dying, the radiant beauty of their essence is revealed in their eyes. When we begin to explore the mysteries and power of our essence, we open to the hidden depths of our potential. We realize that this is where the true sweetness of life dwells. Once we familiarize ourselves with our essence, we can then open more and more to our true life purpose. This is a pretty different conversation from the body-obsessed focus of our culture, isn't it?

When we grasp the fullness of our true essence, our fears and falsities, suffering and struggle for the 'right' image loses importance and ceases to absorb us. Unleashing our true essence allows us to embrace a whole new view of what's possible for our lives. We are not just our bodies and we are most definitely more than the rampage of thoughts and entertaining persuasions that the mind creates. At our fullest, we are radiant, intelligent beings, shining from the inside out.

John O'Donohue claimed that *your essence is the utter 'isness', the utter 'youness' of you.* Your essence is the truest part of who you are, your being-ness. Our challenge is to uncover our true essence and then learn how we can most effectively share it with the world, by way of service and contribution.

Your essence is the radiant inner core of your being. At every age, our body changes. This is inevitable, but there is something unchanging that remains the same throughout all the stages of our lives. Look at one of your baby pictures and then one of you as a child. Now think of yourself today, nearing adulthood. Through all of these phases there is a consistent energy that shines out of your eyes. This unchanging aspect of your being is your essence.

This part of you is shared with everyone you meet, whether you realize it or not, because your essence emanates through you in every moment of your life. Its impact is subtle, yet pervasive and often goes without notice because we have no language to define it. Once you become conscious of your essence, you want to protect it from fire snuffing patterns such as self depreciation, negativity, shame and abuse. The moment you choose to respect and honor your essence, it will naturally magnify in power, opening doors for greater impact on people's lives.

Pause for Reflection

Every living thing has an essence, including people, pets and plants. Let's play for a minute and imagine yourself as a tree, what kind would you be? An animal, what animal would you be? And a bird, what type of bird comes to mind to describe your unique essence?

As you get to know your essence, come up with one word that describes it. Ask your family and friends how they would describe your essence. This will be helpful in understanding yourself, which will assist you in choosing the way in which you will contribute in the world as an adult.

The one word that best describes my essence is:_____.

Can you think of someone who allows his or her essence to freely shine forth?

How do they bring joy, love or inspiration to the world through their unique radiance?

YOUR LIFE PURPOSE

> Vocation is the place where our deep gladness meets the world's deep need. ~ Frederick Buechner

The tricky challenge we are faced with is identifying the unique quality of our essence. We are so accustomed to its light because it has been a part of us since birth, that we have difficulty seeing our own beauty and brilliance. Every person on earth has a unique essence, and therefore, each of us has a unique purpose for being here. One of the keys to living a fulfilling, happy life is discovering your essence and then exploring how you can leverage your essence to best serve the world.

Your life purpose is woven into the fabric of your being. It is the answer to the question "Why am I here?" Within the answer to this timeless question lies the details of your essence and your life purpose.

Discovering the unique qualities of your essence will help you to articulate your life purpose. But these answers to your reason for being here may not arrive immediately. They may take years to unravel. The sooner you begin this inquiry, the sooner you'll discover who you are and what lights you up. And with that kind of clarity, the more excited you'll feel about the vast possibilities for your life.

Not only will this clarity bring you more passion for life, it will help to establish you in your own personal power. There is nothing more powerful than seeing a person who is clear on their 'why' and unabashedly shares their gifts with the world. Their interest in enhancing the world with what they have to offer outweighs any fears of being imperfect or inadequate. From activists to athletes, we've all seen people engaging life with this level of passion and courage, and it's this kind of personal power that inspires and elevates other people's lives.

> When your life is on course with it's purpose, you are at your most powerful. And though you may stumble, you will not fall.[32]

CONCLUSION

As a Girl on Fire, you are gradually assembling the unique pieces of the puzzle of you, which you will continue to discover as you grow. The clues to your true destiny lie in discovering your essence and honoring your inner desires, which usually match your natural gifts. The concept of dharma, or life purpose, teaches us to pursue work in a field that aligns with our

---

[32] Oprah Winfrey, *What I know for Sure*, (Hearst Communications, Inc., 2014), 218

natural gifts, so that our work is not really work, but an opportunity for us to shine our light and playfully share our gifts with the world. When we live in this way, our contribution to the planet has no limits!

Omwork

Create an art form, such as a photo, drawing, or even a physical posture that reflects your true essence. You will have the opportunity to share this next week in our final celebration of you.

Affirmations

I allow my true essence to guide my life, and in return, I receive boundless opportunities.

I know I am most powerful when I live in accordance with my heart's desire.

With each breath, I become more connected to the miraculous universal energy that created me.

Today, I look beyond others shortcomings and acknowledge their true essence.

Personal Additions:

Physical posture

Camel Posture

Mindful Movement Class - Week 11

NOTE: This is the Mindful Movement Class to accompany Week 11. For consistency and ease, we recommend the video series of these classes available at www.GirlOnFire.ca.

Weekly theme – Essence
Opening Pose of your choice, Mandala Breathing Inhale and exhale, gaining a sense of this circular flow, then add inhale and pause at the top, exhale and hold, accentuating the nourishing fullness as well as the cleansing emptiness of life. Now imagine the inhalation drawing energy up your backside, retaining your breath gently at the crown and exhale, feel the energy spill down your front body, holding the outbreath briefly at the pelvic floor before doing it all again with your next breath. The circle is used to represent our life experiences, realizing that everything in the material world is born and so must die as well, where an ending occurs on the circle, there is a beginning right beside it. Let's take this time to acknowledge the work you've done to date, scanning back over the last few months. Notice what if anything, has dropped away from your life since taking this program. Have you experienced a death of sorts? And what about new beginnings, in relationship to yourself, or to others. Any new insights or new feelings you have about your life or your future? Take them with you as you flow. Standing Head rotations Shoulder Rolls Starling Flow Tea Cup Dance Full Body Flow Mandala Namaskara **Feature Posture:** Camel Pose Child's Pose **Partner Posture:** The Falcon Knee to Chest Pose Supine Twist with arm circles Cat Tail Pose Savasana/Relaxation Pose
Reflection
Seated Position with Lotus mudra.

Girl on Fire closing

To acknowledge the three centers of Power, Love and Insight:

Rise to sitting and bring palms together. Lift hands so that thumbs touch the mid eye point and say: *"Guided by insight"*

Now draw hands to heart, one palm on heart center in the middle of the chest and the other palm resting on top of the first hand and say: *"I listen to my heart's desire"*

Now take the top hand and slide it down so it rests on the navel, with the first hand remaining on the heart and say: *"And take positive, powerful action in the world"*

Notes

Week 12 – Celebration

INTO THE WORLD WITH AN UNWAVERING SENSE OF YOU!

In today's society, we are taught that your self worth is contingent on your appearance, your achievements, your shoes, your clothes, your friends etc. Most of us grow up believing that we are deficient in some way and not good enough because we don't measure up to the standards that are impressed upon us day in day out in very subtle but deeply impressionable ways. When we depend on other's approval for our sense of peace and happiness, we are set up to live a life of instability, disappointment and sadness. Remember what this approach to life is called? This is what we call object referred living, striving for the green light from others to tell us that we're okay and lovable. Our self worth is completely dependent on our self-image, the outward image we portray to the world, also known as the ego.

Life as the ego is: fearful, separate from others, self-centered, attached to the material world. In general, we all attempt to label and categorize people based on their outward image, but the moment we do that, we dismiss the true essence of who they really are.

In yoga, there is quite an opposite way of looking at our life. The physical body, which is where we tend to focus all of our attention in this part of the world, is our outer most layer, and furthest from the true essence of who we are. Within our core of our being is a light, which is a spark from the great flame of all creation.

Every living creature possesses the same spark of divine light, from fire flies to lizards. And humans are the only ones who question our self worth and inner beauty. Giraffes don't sit around fretting about whether or not their necks are long enough. Lions don't worry about whether or not their roar is on key. And you can bet that roses don't think twice about the beauty of their blossom, they just bloom!

Did you know that you are an expression of this amazing original light that created the world? Did you know that you and everyone else in the world are incredible beings of light, regardless of the language you speak and the clothes you wear? From this perspective, we live with the awareness that we are all unique and radiant with a special purpose to fulfill.

But this awareness also includes the fact we are imperfect, a continual work in progress and while our lives will contain successes, they will also be speckled with mistakes. It's essential that we allow ourselves to live fully in this way, with resilience, falling into the hole, climbing back out, and standing back up. It's these bounce back moments that will ultimately define the course of our lives, not the mistakes, but our courage to get back on the proverbial horse and engage life again, with our scars, our bumps and our bruises. A Girl on Fire has such a firm belief in herself that even in the midst of mistakes and failures, she never questions her worth, she just trudges forward. This is a true Girl on Fire, a warrior woman.

This belief in yourself, this understanding that you are a spark of brilliance is and will forever be your greatest source of power in your life.

By developing an unwavering sense of self worth as we identify our spiritual essence, we garner the strength to ride the waves of life with grace and optimism. When we live life with the expectation that everything must stay the same, we live rigidly, attempting to control every facet of life. When we live with the awareness of the one unchanging law of the universe, the law of change itself, knowing that everything in the material world changes, we learn to flow with the river. Attempting to control life is like swimming upstream, living with purpose and resilience is like cruising downstream with a paddle, you're clear on your desired outcome (the paddle) and you allow the current to guide your way, accepting the occasional surprise.

Time capsule Letter to the you in five years time

The opportunity to step into your greatness is always knocking. New friends are on their way. The ideas you need in order to fulfill your dreams are finding you. Everyday is a fresh start. Every moment is another chance to love yourself more. Your life is becoming brighter. You are feeling lighter. Love is rising up. You are quietly, inwardly preparing for all the new opportunities coming your way. Others will call you lucky. Your parents will be amazed. Look out world, this Girl on Fire is stirring... a giant flame is waking up.

A Message from Jenny

My dear friend,

You made it and I'm so proud of you. But the journey is not over, in fact, it's truly just begun. Not only do you have the freedom to live your life authentically, but you also have a responsibility to do so now.

The Universe has a way of letting us know the things we need to know when we're ready. The moment I realized that I had a responsibility to share my light with the world occurred during my second trip to India.

I was still a fairly inexperienced traveler, having lived a rather protected life in small town New Brunswick. The developing world was so foreign to me that it was much like stepping onto another planet. But over the weeks of living and practicing yoga there, I grew more relaxed and familiar with the wild pace of life.

One day, as I was sitting in the back seat of a rickety old rickshaw on my way to my comfortable hotel room, I had an exchange that would change my life forever. As we slowed to yield to traffic ahead (a strange and rare occurrence in India), I peered out my back window to catch a glimpse of a community of people who lived beneath tarps and sold watermelons along the roadside.

In a moment of beautiful synchronicity, an older woman caught my eye and somehow commanded my full attention. Within about three seconds, her intense gaze looked right inside my soul. As if speaking out loud, she said, "Go do something with your life, for yourself and for all of us. We are confined here, but you are not. Go make a difference!" And then she was gone, as we lurched forward through the intersection.

I knew this connection was meant to deliver a message to me, and I was both deeply moved and utterly terrified. This meant I would have to hurdle the limiting beliefs that kept me small, but oh so safe. This meant that I would have to listen to and obey the vision within my heart, and that was scary.

Showing up differently in the world is indeed scary because we don't really know how it's all going to shake down. Will we be accepted? Successful? Happy? But here's the catch; we'll never truly know unless we go for it. Well I went for it and I'm so glad I did.

A few weeks ago I was cuddling with my girls. As I held them each in one arm, I was overwhelmed with love and spontaneously said, "Oh wow, this is such an amazing moment. If only I had known as a troubled teen, the joy and the love that was waiting for me here." No matter who you are and what struggles you face today, the same joy and love awaits you.

As our program comes to a close, I want to send you off with my wishes for you as a Girl on Fire Graduate:

Self-awareness

That you commit to understanding yourself and learn to be with yourself compassionately and gently, with the awareness that as a teenager you *will* likely make impulsive decisions, take risks and make mistakes. Despite that, you remain lovable and you will be loved always.

Self worth

When you see an advertisement with a grossly underweight, over-sexualized model draped over a new shiny car that you'll be able to observe the instinctive desire to look like her and take a slow, deep breath, remembering that your reason for being here goes far beyond the role of car sales and sexual arousal.

Confidence

That knowing your worth, you will confidently advocate for yourself, seeking out proper support when you need it. Like the gasoline that enables a vehicle to move, confidence is the necessary fuel that enables you to fulfill your destiny. The people who have made a difference in the world didn't have all the answers to their plan before they started. What they did have was the confidence in themselves to figure it out as they went along. Remember: fake it 'til you become it!

Discernment

You are a Girl on Fire now and with your newly awakened sight, you practice discernment with every choice you make. May you carefully choose friends and lovers who align with your moral code and may your lifestyle choices nourish your stream of wellbeing. Remember, the best way to develop discernment is to learn from your mistakes.

Resiliency

Like a bamboo tree, you live out your life with deep roots connected to nature and to love, while yielding to the storms that strike all of us. The human race has survived amazing hardship; you have this fortitude in your DNA, just read your family history! Remember, life is not about waiting for the storm to pass, but learning to dance in the rain.

Discipline

This can be a tough one I know, and at times it might feel easier to just give up. But discipline is required to fulfill any dream. Your life will unfold and time will pass no matter what. My hope is that in twenty years you'll be enjoying the gratification of hard work in the direction of your dreams, not wallowing in a pool of regret. Devote so much of your life to becoming your best that you have no time to criticize others or complain.

Optimism

Instead of falling into the typical narrow-minded, negative perspective that the adult mind can sink into, you stay on the sunny side of life with the help of the 3 A's (admit, allow, act). There's always something to laugh about, always. Fuel your faith in a Universal Love Intelligence everyday, and assume the belief that the whole world is on your side, conspiring on your behalf!

Contentment

That you drop the desire to be anyone else but you and take time each day to appreciate the gift that is your life; giving thanks for your body, your creativity and your abilities. Contentment is the ability to fully appreciate where you are, while you're there.

Connection

The next time you dismiss a request for connection in favor of time on the screen, remember that our main purpose here as human beings is to connect and grow in love and respect for one another. Always know that in the presence of an open heart, the miraculous is possible.

Essence

The you that is you has never been before and will never be again. Hidden beneath the layers of your heart is your unique essence, which holds the answers to your special life purpose that only you can fulfill. Don't waste time on the stuff that drains you. Listen for what lights you up and take one step at a time in that direction. The path may be vague and you may stray off course, but keep listening. Say yes to opportunities that feel good and eventually you'll find yourself standing in the middle of your sweetest, deepest dreams.

These are my wishes for you.
Be Love, Be You, Be a Girl on Fire!

Jenny K

Notes

Girl on Fire Reflection Questions

1) Has the Girl on Fire Program changed your outlook on life? If so, explain.
2) Please indicate whether this program met your expectations and your satisfaction on a scale of 1 to 10, ten being "Well satisfied."

1	5	10
Not met expectations		Well satisfied

3) Has the Girl on Fire Program helped you manage your stress? If so, explain.
4) What did you like best about the Girl on Fire Program? Please explain.
5) Which of the 10 Core Competencies of the Girl on Fire Program has made the biggest impact on you? Explain how and/or why?
    - Self-awareness
    - Self-esteem
    - Confidence
    - Resiliency
    - Discernment
    - Discipline
    - Optimism
    - Contentment
    - Compassion
    - Essence
6) What part of the Girl on Fire Program has had the biggest effect on your life? Explain.
7) What strategy or strategies have you learned that you will continue to use in the future and why?
8) What would you like to change about the Girl on Fire Program? Explain.
9) Would you recommend the Girl on Fire Program to other high school females? Explain why or why not?

Appendix A – Abhyanga Instructions

Ayurveda espouses the value of living in harmony with nature and up until a century ago, we spent 90% of our time outdoors, surrounded by the elements.

Today however, many of us spend 90% of our time inside, insulating ourselves from nature's pharmacy. In the process of becoming estranged from the natural world, our current lifestyles expose us to unprecedented levels of toxins. From foods that stay on shelves for months, to industry pollutants, to the constant barrage of violent images on TV, humanity now faces a whole host of new illnesses, allergies and mental health conditions.

Under the burden of toxic influences and the stress of over-scheduled lives, our systems can easily slide out of balance. When this happens, we can experience a range of symptoms such as anxiety, fatigue, confusion, aggression and hopelessness.

With our strong commitment to supporting your optimal health, we've created a line of Breathing Space Ayurvedic Oils designed to infuse your daily life with the healing benefits of nutrient-rich plant extracts. These oils will help to re-establish balance in your unique body/mind type, or dosha, known as Vata, Pitta or Kapha.

By balancing our doshas with Yoga and Abhyanga (self-massage) we can quickly enhance our wellbeing, bringing clarity, balance, calm and enjoyment back into our lives.

The best part? Abhyanga massage only takes a few minutes each day!

BENEFITS OF ABHYANGA MASSAGE

- Nourishes the skin
- Removes fatigue
- Balances our doshas
- Eliminates waste products and detoxifies
- Releases age-reversing happy hormones
- Increases flexibility
- Boosts immunity
- Lubricates joints
- Increases body temperature
- Regulates every system of the body

How to do Abhyanga

Take a moment before you begin to invoke an attitude of reverence for your body. Aligning your intention with the healing vibration of the essential oils will optimize the impact on your body, mood and self-esteem. This is your time to give your body love and tender care.

On a towel or bath mat, begin by rubbing oil into your scalp and hair. Move to the forehead, cheeks, chin and ears and then massage down the neck, shoulders and arms. When massaging the arms and legs, use circular motions at the joints and long strokes on the upper and lower limbs.

Using the whole hand, gently use circular motions on the chest and belly. Massaging the belly in a clockwise direction (up the right side, down the left) will encourage elimination. Reach both hands around to massage the spine and hips as best you can (or enlist support☺). Move down the legs, circling around the knees and ankles, while rubbing up and down on the long bones. Complete your self-massage by tending to the feet and toes.

Sit quietly for a few minutes, taking deep, soothing breaths before stepping into your bath or shower (be careful not to slip!). While the bath helps to remove excess oils and toxins that are brought to the skin's surface, in the dry fall and winter seasons, you can leave your oils on throughout the day.

In the morning, you can massage more vigorously to energize your system. If you're preparing for sleep, slow, strong motions will help relax your body and quiet your mind.

If you are a dry vata, you may see great benefit to both starting and finishing your day with this practice. If you are a kapha, you may find that every other day or less is sufficient, as your skin's oil content is already high. Remember, as we age, we all become more vata.

Pressed for time? Just massaging oils into the feet, belly and scalp will help to keep your system nourished all day.

And don't forget to hydrate from the inside out, with 2L of water consumption a day!

Abhyanga and Yoga

Applying Abhyanga oils before yoga can greatly enhance your practice. Just be sure to wear clothing that you don't mind getting a bit oily and lay a practice towel down on top of your yoga mat.

Appendix B – References and Recommendations

The following list of materials are mentioned in this manual. For further study in specific topics please enjoy these selections.

Amy Cuddy, TED talk, "Your Body Language Shapes Who You Are" https://www.ted.com/talks/amy_cuddy_your_body_language_shapes_who_you_are

Brene Brown, *Daring Greatly*, (Penguin Random House, 2012)

Carol Dweck, *Mindset: The New Psychology of Success*, (Ballentine Books, 2008)

Caroline Myss, *Anatomy of the Spirit* (Three Rivers Press, 1996)

Clarissa Pinkola Estes, Power of the Crone (Sounds True Inc. audio)

Cyndi Dale, *Energetic Boundaries*, (Sounds True Inc., 2011)

Christiane Northrup, M.D., *Mother-Daughter Wisdom*, (Bantam trade paperback edition April 2006)

Frances E. Jensen, *The Teenage Brain*, (Colins, Jan 2015)

Kristin Neff, PhD, *Self-Compassion: Stop Beating Yourself Up and Leave Insecurity Behind* (HarperCollins, 2011)

Leonard Sax, *Girls On The Edge*, (Basic Books, 2011)

Lisa M. Schab, *The Anxiety Workbook for Teens*, (Raincoast Books, 2008)

Nischala Joy Devi, *The Healing Path of Yoga*, (Harmony June 6, 2000)

Oprah Winfrey, *What I know for Sure*, (Hearst Communications, Inc., 2014)

Sherry Turkle, *Alone Together*, (Basic Books, 2011)

Shiva Rea, *Tending the Heart Fire*, (Sounds True Inc., 2014)

Yoga Journal and Timothy McCall, *Yoga as Medicine* (Penguin Random House, 2007)

Appendix C – Resources

The following two images are used in conjuction with:
    Week 9 – Perfection vs Love, the butterfly
    Week 11 – Your Life Purpose, the flower

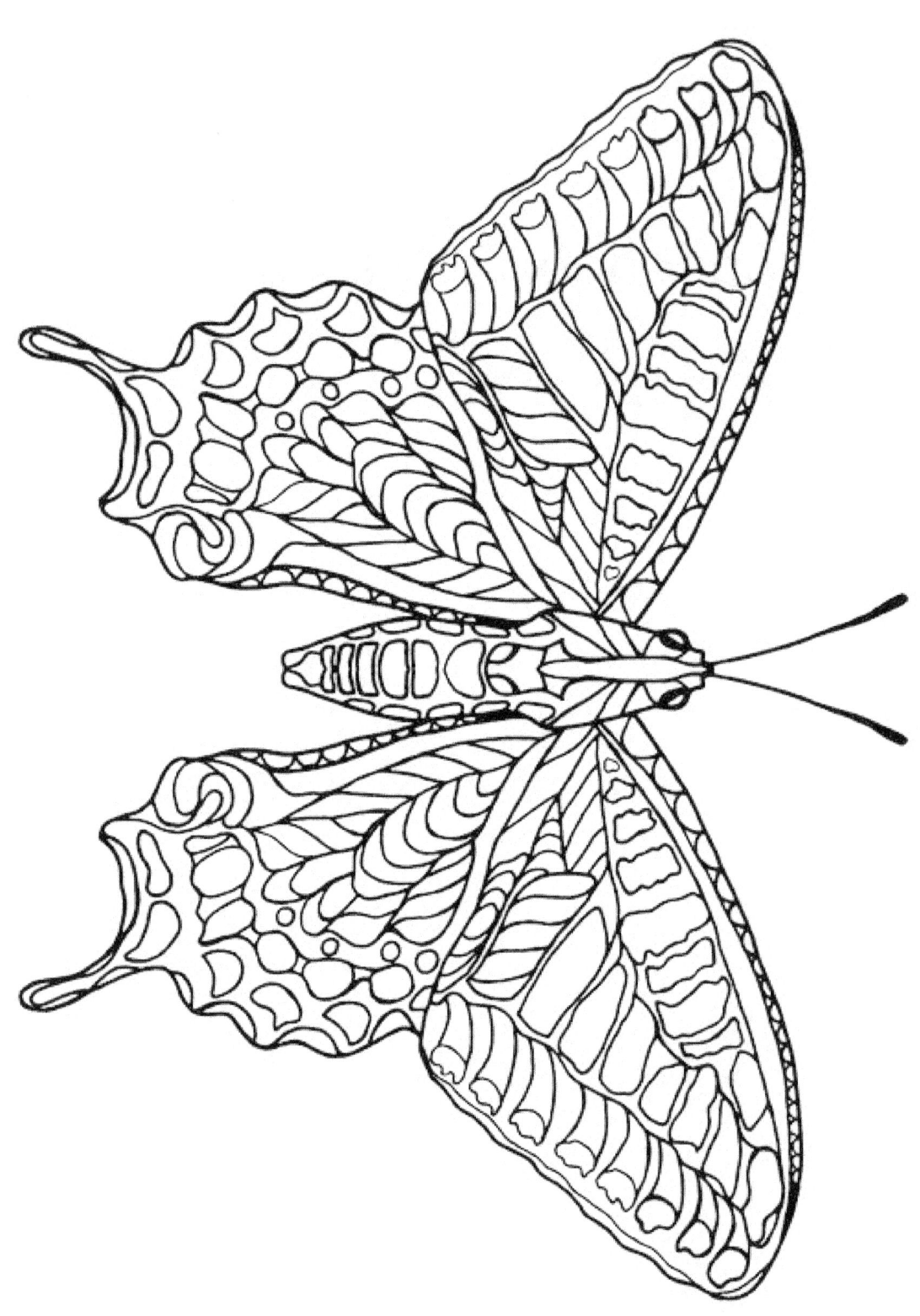

www.ingramcontent.com/pod-product-compliance
Lightning Source LLC
Chambersburg PA
CBHW080411300426
44113CB00015B/2480